Best w

Around the
White Peak

High Peak Hunt at the Waterloo,
Taddington 1910

Compiled by Sheila Hine
with additions by Claude Fearns

Front cover: Mr Redfern from Wormhill at Miller's Dale Quarry c.1925.

Back cover: The Well Yard at Flagg and Threshing at Great Longstone.

CHURNET VALLEY BOOKS
1 King Street, Leek, Staffordshire. ST13 5NW 01538 399033
www.leekbooks.co.uk
© Sheila Hine and Churnet Valley Books 2007
ISBN 978-1-904546 64 1

Tunstead 1935.

The steam shovel 1948.

CONTENTS

Acknowledgements

Thanks to all who have contributed in any way, either stories or photos and memorabilia.
Thanks to Peak District National Park Authority for a contribution towards the costs.

FOR OTHER PHOTOS: Tarmac, Buxton Lime & Cement.
Tony Hill, Angela Taylor (John & Julie Gregory, Wilde family, Taylor family, Les Wilshaw).

At Wormhill. Blessing of the Well 1951. Festival of Britain.

Knotbury Sam was a smallholder at Waterswallows.
He also worked in the Tunstead Quarry in the 1920s.

Bill Gregory's mum, Gladys, with her white Wyandottes.

Bill Gregory

I have been involved with a lot of people who have researched and investigated this area over the years. This is a synopsis, in my own words, with what I've learnt from them about Blackwell and this farm, Blackwell Hall Farm. John Barnett, an archaeologist working from the Peak Park did a survey about ten years ago, paid for by English Heritage and he came up with fifty sites of archaeological and historical interest on this one farm, which is quite amazing.

I'll start way back in the Stone Age; right down in the north-east corner of the farm is a little cave; they think that is a rock shelter where the early inhabitants of this area, who were hunter-gatherers, would shelter near a water supply - around five thousand years ago.

Then we come forward in time to Neolithic people or Celts. They were the first farmers; they kept livestock and grew crops. This had evolved from the Middle East and gradually over several thousand years come to Europe and Britain. The evidence of that is in the Celtic fields, little fields about as large as a big room, which they ploughed with a stick, throwing the stones to the sides. So there are heaps of stones all the way round. They were probably cultivated for two or three thousand years. Quite a few flint implements have been found over the years.

Moving on from the Celts, there is thought to be a Bronze Age burial, down at the north end of the farm. Moving on from there, there was a mound which the archaeologists dug and found evidence of the Iron Age. There were squares underground, all done in basalt, which may have been of religious significance.

Then we move to the Roman or Romano-British period. On the top of the hill overlooking the River Wye, there's a settlement, where you can see the little fields and where the circular huts were. It was dug by a team of archaeologists from Sheffield, led by Harry Lane, quite a character. He had been in the original SAS, Colonel Stirling's SAS, formed in the North African desert during the war. He was very fit and he married one of his students, she was nineteen, he was seventy-two. They gave us demonstrations of Ju-Jitsu - Harry could throw her about and she could throw him about as well.

He found lots of artefacts, querns, pottery shards and they found a skeleton; not very deep underground; because it's quite rocky, there's only about a foot of soil. They said it was a unique burial; it was a girl and she'd got lead nodules in each eye socket and a necklace of lead nodules around her neck. They had people from Oxford come and look, it was quite significant. They took the bones to the Home Office pathologist and they said she was about seventeen and had died, probably in childbirth, about 400AD.

Moving on through the Saxon period, from about 450AD to the Norman Conquest; Saxons, Ancient Britons, Angles and Jutes all mixed up together. There is a biggish field down there, which is terraced. They say that was done in the Saxon period and they would have used baskets, wooden shovels, antler picks and a tremendous amount of hard work. Land must have been in short supply and there must have been a lot of people about if it was worthwhile doing all that work to get some flat land. It's supposed to be one of the best preserved in the north of England. There is another one at Priestcliffe, but not as extensive. Some people say that they grew vines on them, the climate may have been warmer then, but ours is north-facing. There is also evidence of the Celtic fields running under these terraces.

The Normans were a pretty brutal lot and may have said to the Saxons around here, 'We want this land and if you object, we'll chop your heads off!' So it was all taken over by the Normans; this area, Buxton, Chelmorton, Monyash was given to William Peveril, who resided at Peveril Castle, Castleton. He was William the Conqueror's eldest illegitimate son and was a bit of a naughty boy, so he thought he would never go to Heaven unless he did something about it. He decided to give these estates, or at least the income from them, to the monks of Lenten Priory at Nottingham, about 1100AD. He gave them two thirds of the income; tithes of livestock, grain etc; one third went to the Dean and Chapter of Lichfield.

It was a bone of contention for 400 years. Each thought the other was having more than they should. In the 1300s, the Dean of Lichfield, who had Tideswell Church, heard the monks were on their way to challenge their share, so they got all these animals into Tideswell Church. The monks rolled up and battered on the doors, broke in and blood was spilt in the church, both animal and human. The church was closed until the Pope had done something about it.

This sort of thing went on for years. Then Henry VIII came along and confiscated all the lands belonging to the monks and distributed it about among his pals. The Cavendish family got this estate, eventually Sir William Cavendish, who married Bess of Hardwick. She had great plans and wanted to build a stately home here. In the *Derbyshire Archaeological Journal* of 1965 there are plans of it, which exist in the Architect's Institute in London. It was a smaller version of Hardwick Hall. She rented the estate from the family for 17s 6d a year.

The Cavendish family held it for over 100 years until Charles I's time and the civil war. Most of the estates of the people who'd supported the Royalist cause were confiscated. In the case of Blackwell, there was a family who had lived here for centuries. They were called Blackwell, I think they took their name from the well down the dale which comes out from basalt rocks, and is still called the black well. They had been stewards of the estate from time immemorial and were important people. They bought and sold land on behalf of the owners and collected rents, put buildings up and had always been good and trusted people.

They hadn't got much money, so they went up to Scotland to borrow money from the Scottish Earls, the Earl of Crawford and the Earl of Haddington. So they bought this estate, but there were some mistakes made in the Deed of Transfer, it may have been jiggery-pokery and when Charles II was restored to the throne, the Cavendish family claimed it back. The poor Blackwell family had to take their case to the House of Lords. There are records of getting to London from here, which took two weeks, and they had to take all these people, schoolmasters and all sorts with them to support the case. It cost a fortune and to cut a long story short, they lost their case and went bankrupt for £150,000 in 1680 - maybe £20 million nowadays. That was the end of them, the old hall fell into ruins and the estate was run down.

So it was back to the Cavendish family, the Portland branch. They owned it till 1825, when they came to an agreement with the Chatsworth Cavendish family, who held some ground next to the Portland estate, and they did a swap.

There is a Cavendish map produced in 1631 which shows that Blackwell was divided into strips then, right from the top of the hill above the A6, down to the River Wye. Long narrow strips and I think they swapped strips, so that good farmers and poor farmers all had a level playing field. That map is in the Shire Hall at Nottingham.

The Cavendish family held the estate until the 1950s when a lot of land had to be sold to pay death duties. Most tenants brought their farms very cheaply and that's how our family came to own this farm. When you think about it, it's only had four owners since the Norman Conquest.

There are two large lead mines on the farm, one is the Slitherford Stewards mine, opened in 1763 and the other is the Saint Peters mine, opened in 1805. There are other small mines not recorded. In the old farmyard here, the oldest range of buildings is thought to be 17th century

Cleaning out the reservoir at Blackwell Hall mid-1930s.

Left to Right: Edward Crawford, Mike McCann (Irish labourer), Bill Gregory Snr, Wilfred Mettam, Ralph Millward.

At Moor Grange, Mum and Dad.

At Moor Grange, Dad.

across the top of the yard. All the mortar is lime mortar; there is no coal ash in it; that's how it's dated. The mines in Buxton were opened in the 1700s. All the rest of the buildings have used lime-ash - 'ess' they call it - mixed with the lime, which made it much harder.

This range on the north side of the yard was built about 1803. When we were altering the building, there was a through barn, a threshing barn, where you could open the big doors at each side and on a windy day, they used to throw it up and it blew the chaff out of the grain. There was a threshing floor in there, which was a floor with no nails in it, just bolted through with long bolts. When we moved it out, there were initials carved underneath and the date 1803.

The building which is now the Farming Life Centre was built around 1860 and was the stable block. A cow once got up the stairs onto the loft which was pretty rotten, creaking and with holes appearing. There was a lady working here at the time, Maggie Bowen, who was Welsh. She said, *'I'll get it down for you.'* And she got a bucket with some corn in, went up and came backwards down the stairs and this cow slowly followed her down. She was quaking; it could have leapt on top of her at any moment.

There is an interesting building up at the back, a Victorian sheepfold. There was a shepherd's cabin with a fire in the corner. We keep young stock in it now. My mother can remember going up; they had a resident shepherd, an old chap and they used to roast chestnuts on his fire when they were kids.

Fairey did an agricultural survey in 1820. A man lived here then called Joshua Linguard, who was a pioneer in all sorts of things. One thing was liming the land. At that time they burnt lime in these beehive kilns - pretty crude and inefficient. He built a kiln shaped like a boat in which the fire went round and as it was drawn out, the fire followed you round. You put a layer of coal, a layer of stone, a layer of coal, a layer of stone etc. It's still there, it was six times more efficient. The family built some properties up at Priestcliffe Ditch, they were Sheffield butchers then.

The chap that followed them was Arthur Heathcote and this trough in the yard was put in then, they had quarries at Stanton. They were here until 1866, when the Moores came. Then in 1892, my grandfather came. Mr Moore said to my grandfather, *'They promised me new winders in the house in '66 an' they anner dun 'em yet.'* And those windows were still there until we replaced them about ten years ago; so you can tell what draughts we had!

Grandfather came here in 1892 after having two years at Manor Farm. He died in 1932 and my father went into partnership with my uncle and they farmed it until my father died in 1947 aged 45. He got pneumonia in the big snow and kept working when he should have taken time off. That's farming isn't it? I took over in 1959.

On my mother's side, we originate from the Mortons at Brierlow Grange. They had 14 children and reared them all; two of them went to America in 1840, in the covered wagons, and ripped a farm out of the bush. I've got a letter which one of them wrote back to his brother. The first thing they did - they were staunch Methodists - was to build a chapel and a stable for the horses and a place to store the turnips. He said, *'We're quite close to the Missouri River, so we'll be well placed to send food back to Ingland.'* And you can tell how near the frontier they were, they'd been to chapel one Sunday and the Indians had been to his neighbour's house and killed his wife and all his children and set the place afire. The family is still on the same farm today.

My great, great grandmother, Hannah Morton, she married Tom Percival at Chelmorton and they went to live at Far Ditch Farm and had a family, the eldest my great grandma called Anne. She became pregnant with her boyfriend, so a wedding had to be organised quickly, because Methodists didn't do things like that! Tragically, he was killed before my grandfather

Bill Gregory Snr and Jnr 1935.

RIGHT:
Bill Gregory,
with Hedley
Cooper
at Blackwell.

BELOW:
At Moor Grange,
Nelly Percival

Joseph Skidmore ploughing

was born. He had a thrashing business in the winter-time and a merry-go-round in the summer-time; steam-driven and he got his leg in the thrashing machine and died from his injuries.

So grandfather didn't have a father and he lived with his mother and grandmother, because his grandfather had also died very young. They ran the farm, then his mother met another man, but my grandfather didn't like him. They fought on one or two occasions. When he married my grandmother they moved to Manor Farm in 1890 and to here in 1892, when John Mycock's grandfather took over Manor farm.

They were a huge family, the Mycocks, my mother's mother's family. Mother had 72 cousins. Her mother was a 7th child and my mother was a 7th child, my grandparents lost four before they reared one. So she was the 7th child of a 7th child and they are supposed to have all sorts of mystical powers; she could water divine and things like that.

Bill Gregory Snr seed-sowing at Blackwell Hall

My dad's side, the Gregorys, originated from Coplow Dale; my great great grandfather had a little lead mine there. He came to Taddington around 1860. Dad was the youngest of seven; he had five brothers and one sister, his mother died when he was five and his father died when he was nine, so Aunty Maude, the second child brought them all up. She died not long ago, aged 100. She never married; she was housekeeper for all sorts of people.

To sum up, in 1950 30 people lived in Blackwell; 2 were retired. There were 7 houses, 6 full-time farmers, 1 part-time & 140 cows. Now there are 31 people, 10 retired, 13 houses, 3 full-time, 2 part-time farmers. The parish area is 800 acres; with 2 dairy farms with 450 cows.

Carting water from Miller's Dale

George Gregory, on the left, at Moor Grange 1930. Mark Bown & Bill Gregory Snr at Moor Grange 1930.

At Moor Grange

At Blackwell Hall, late 1940s. Mee's delivering cabbage plants.

At Blackwell Hall, Bill Gregory Snr and Jnr.

Local cycling club c.1900, with Mr and Mrs George Drewry taking part, on the lawn at Blackwell Hall.

Bill and Geoff Gregory 1938.

Chelmorton Tales - Claude

I had not been going to Chelmorton School for long and as I set off one morning, there were wisps of snow on the wind. Mum didn't know whether to let me go or not, but I went. We lived on an out of the way farm called The Burrs. When I got to school, I hung my coat up in the porch and changed my wellies for pumps and then went into school to my place, putting my bag with books and sandwiches in, on a shelf under the desk. There was also a tin in it with a lid on each end which held cocoa and sugar. We gave these tins to the teacher to make our mid morning or lunchtime drink.

The first thing after assembling in the big room was to take the register. The headmistress, Mrs Waterfall, welcomed us to another exiting day. (Very exiting for some of us!) Next came prayers, then Miss Makinson read some scripture from the Old Testament. I liked the Old Testament; I could go into a dreamworld and imagine I was back in those times. Then Miss McKevvitt took hymns and after that we settled down to some real work, maths or English.

By 11 o'clock our cocoa was ready, made from water boiled in a big kettle on the coal fire. We sat at long desks, 6-10 in a row; we each had inkwells, but no-one used a pen in the infants. The ink for the others was made at school; one of the teachers got a big jug of water, a jar of blue dye and a glass container which held about 4 pints. She half-filled it with water, then added powder until the right colour was gained. It was then put into small jugs and taken to fill the inkwells, which were white pots sunk into the desktop, one for each pupil.

The afternoon was made up of general studies. 3pm came; we put our books away and trooped to the cloakroom door. The teachers waited until we were all ready and dressed to go, but when we got outside we found it had snowed welly deep. We were met by the caretaker, who held us behind the safety railings because the snowplough was coming up the road driven by Mr Mellor with his shire horses. We waited for him to go past but he didn't, he turned into Common Lane, stopped and asked for me. *'Come on wi' thee'* he said, putting me on a long seat on the back of the snowplough used by the roadmen.

Off we went and I remember stopping at the end of the Burrs lane where Mr Mellor picked me up and carried me through the deep snow at the edge of the road. He put me down into snow which came above my knees and said, *'Now go straight home, don't stop for nothing at all - off you go.'* It was tiring walking in snow up to your knees; although it was soft and powdery my wellies were soon full. When I'd got 150 yards down the road, I turned round to see him watching me; we waved to each other and I carried on down the lane. He moved off up Coalpit Lane to a point where he could see me get to where mum could see me at the top stile. Anyway, that was me home safe and my first contact with a snowplough.

For me it was a great day when granddad came to stay with us. On winter days he would say, *'Get your jobs done and we'll have an early night.'* After seeing to my hens, my job was getting a bundle of kindling sticks for fire lighting to place on a shelf above the oven to dry overnight.

As I got older the jobs grew into getting the buckets of coal and logs in; filling the boiler at the side of the fire with water - it only needed topping up because as we ladled hot water out, we usually put some back. Then fetch two buckets of clean drinking water for the house and a bucket of trough water if we needed to cool anything.

With dad being at work, granddad would do his jobs, looking after the cattle and pigs. He would milk the cow last, so the last thing to go into the house was the milk; and we were ready for a siege! When dad got in, he took his coat off and hung it up to dry, then put the heavy curtain across the door and a bag across the bottom to keep the draught out. We washed our hands in an enamel bowl on the stone sink; there was a clean Hessian sack to dry our hands on - we kept the towel for drying our faces.

Ma had put the dinner on the table. After eating, she cleared the table and dad made the fire up for the night. First he cleared the burnt ash out with the poker, then he put a good shovel of coal on, then one or two logs to be topped up with half a bucket of slack, which was very small coal down to dust. There was a great deal of smoke going up the chimney until the flames broke through from the burning fire below making a cheerful blaze.

When I was little, granddad would sit me on his knee and tell tales or teach me naughty little songs which he persuaded me to sing when mother's relations came to visit. They were posh and grandad thought it was hilarious to see the shocked looks on their faces; he would laugh till tears ran down his cheeks.

Old Mick lived opposite the post office by himself. His fire was always smoking because his chimney wanted sweeping and his windows were full of great big cobwebs. He always had a big cat on guard in case he dropped anything edible - he didn't feed it as such, it had to catch its own food, so the house was free from rats and mice.

He didn't believe in mowing machines or machinery of any kind; he thought they were the devil's creation. All he had was a good scythe and stone, a wooden hay rake - probably made at Longnor Mill, where they were made the whole year round and sent in bundles to local markets - a hay fork, bonny rake, brush, shovel, muck fork, spade and wheelbarrow.

His season started in early spring when he wheeled the muck out from his two cows and followers into the nearby meadow and tipped it in heaps in rows. He might have cadged a load to do his far field down Coalpit Lane. He spread it by hand, then he got a thorn bush, just big enough for him to pull, which he dragged over the ground to break and spread the muck further. As he got older, he had lads helping to pull it.

Old Mick

Come mowing time, he would sharpen his scythe and set about mowing the near field, helped by the blacksmith. Then shake it out by hand for 3 days in good weather, then rake it into rows, then put the rows into heaps or 'cocks' ready for carting. Then his method was unusual; he put it on tripods making 'cobs' 8 or 9 feet high and 6 feet across the base. The tripod was made of hazel or ash poles. These cobs were left in the field till needed in winter. This way of building them seemed weatherproof - we once bought some off him and it was good stuff, though he didn't usually mow until September after all the seed had dropped; those meadows were full of flowers and herbs. The top two feet of the cob was finished with green grass which got hot and sweated down to form a waterproof cap.

Sometimes one or two of us local children would visit him; one of our mothers would send him a sandwich or two or scone or cake. He put them carefully into a tin to eat later, putting the lid on securely to stop the 'little people' getting at them - so we always thought that he was Irish. We sat by his smoky fire and he told us tales. As we looked at the fire, layers of soot had built up on the bars and would sometimes break loose and curl up. Then the heat caught them and they'd fly off up the chimney. The older lads called them bogarts but Mick said that Irish bogarts were an evil spirit that lived in the bogs.

King Sterndale School 1903, with Miss Bagshaw.
Children: Back, 4th from left Jim Fearns, 5th Dan Chapman. Front, middle Charles Fearns.

Workers at Blackwell Mill Quarry 1920s. Jack Wilde, back left end, ran the Post Office at Wormhill.

Alison Wilton

My great granddad Chapman originated from Tideswell and was a lot older than great grandma, 20 years in fact. They had a child out of wedlock; granddad Dan was 7 or 8 before they married which was very frowned on then.

My granny, Harriet Longden came from Peak Forest. She worked for Ferrantis at Stockport and came to work at King Sterndale Hall for the Pickford family where she got in with our family who also worked there and who became her mother-in-law and sister-in-law. She used to do the hand-washing of the petticoats and things like that.

Great granddad worked on the railway and got his arm caught in the railway buffers, so ended up with only one arm. Great grandma used to walk from Cowdale, where they lived, to King Sterndale to clean the school and then go back there again at night and look after the cows at home as well. People talk well of her even now and she's been dead over 50 years. A plane once came down near King Sterndale and she was intrigued to know what had happened to the pilot - *'Wheer's t' driver?'*

Dad and my uncle Arthur started keeping lorries at Chelmorton in the late 40s; they ran tippers carting stone, 2 churn wagons, a council wagon and a breakdown wagon.

There were ash pits at Town End where I lived and I was a 'tip rat' always rooting to see what I could find. We kept finding these brass plates; one said First Prize-March 19th 1881 - Peterborough. This is where the National Shire show is held and Mark Dicken told us the story that a famous Shire horse called Norfolk Hero had been kept at Town Head and walked around to mares and when he died they'd buried him with his harness on. Anyway some years ago when we were burying a pig we found the remains of a horses back legs with harness so it was right what they told us - I wish I'd listened more.

My mum died when I was little, and so I spent a lot of time at the Cliff Farm, the home of the Gould family. On a Sunday morning as a treat we had thick bread, toasted, spread with brown residue out of the meat tin or if there was none of that, then Bovril. Then cold dripping on top and then cold sliced potatoes with salt and pepper - just lovely!

I have some ground at Chelmorton which we call 'Old Micks' and dad said that when Old Mick got infirm, they took him to the workhouse in Bakewell and they took him on a chair because he was covered in fleas.

Bagshawes were carpenters and joiners at Chelmorton; they did the joinery when Orient Lodge was built in the 1890s. The buildings of the Shire horse stud there were all tiled and they had like a railway line round them to take the food and stuff round. Mr Samuel Swann Brittain had it built; he was known as S.S. It was a very grand place, they were very wealthy for a while, their money was in tea and coffee plantations. Mrs Brittain was Egyptian and wore a yashmak. It was said that he spoke seven languages. My husband's granddad said when they had a sale there just after the first war, they had lots of stuffed animals and no-one wanted them so lads took them onto the common and burnt them. They eventually lost all their money and left and the bailiff, Mr Bingham took the farm over. At a sale there in 1977, my father bought two gate stumps which are now at Chelmorton Institute.

Dan Chapman's diary

Granddad Chapman kept a diary every day. He was born in 1895 and worked at Blackwell Mill Quarry, filling stone. In 1944 he would be 49. Because his wife, my grandma (mam), worked

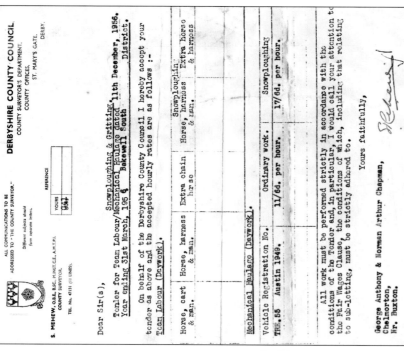

The Chapman's tender for snow ploughing 1956

LEFT: Tony and Arthur
Chapman's snow plough outside
the 'stute in Chelmorton, 1950.

Snow at
Chelmorton

Charabanc trip from Pyle's Garage Buxton in the 1920s. Mr & Mrs Frank Peach are standing left at the back.

BELOW:
Haymaking at Cowdale 1914. Uncle Norman 2nd from left. Gt. Aunt Nance, Forrester the dog and Grandma Chapman on the load. Great Grandma Chapman far right.

Orient Lodge.

The glasshouses before demolition in 1970s.

The glasshouses.

Samuel Swann
Brittain.

Orient Lodge
with Stud Farm.

Travelling shire stallion in Ashwood Dale pre WWI. Probably Grandma Chapman's brother holding the halter.

Bill Skidmore on tractor, Jim (Biddy) in field.

LEFT: Tony Chapman at High Stool.

in service, she was always cleaning and during the war, if there were any black market dealings, she HAD to have soap. They lived in a cottage at the top of Chelmorton near the church. Uncle Arthur was away in the forces. The War Memorial Institute at Chelmorton (the 'stute') was built on land donated by Mrs Bertha Housley on the condition that no alcohol was to be bought or sold on the premises. It was where the young men of the area got together to play cards and billiards and socialise. The smithy was also a great meeting place where gossip was exchanged. Details in italics are for clarification.

Dan

4th Feb 1944 Freezing, very cold. Leg still bad, up in the night. Had front tyre off *(car)*. Down smithy afternoon. Threshing at B.Head. Down Bushies *(Jack Robinson)*. Called D. Mycocks. Lads ENSA 'stute. Mams back bad, very tired.

8th Feb Windy and cold. Down smithy, saw Walter Redfern. Thresher at Woodies. Arthur got port wine compensation from ICI. Lads 'stute. Mam, a bad cold and throat. Leg and hip still bad. Mangle roller gone.

Sat 22nd July Fine, filled 5 *(trucks of stone)* Called Calton *(farm where Slaters lived)*. Saw Swindell's fresh horse. Buxton with mam; hair cut. Gilmans for gooseberries. Buried Michael Percival *(old Mick)*. Paid Biddy *(butcher Jim Skidmore)* Arthur took chisels to be sharpened.

23rd August Dirty day, home with cold. 4 bags coal. Paris and Marseille liberated. Mam cleaned pantry and cupboard. Roumania peace with Russia. Tony committee meeting 'stute.

4th Sept dirty day, filled 8, rake bad. Called Calton. Paid rent. Woodward bought Mick's ground. Tony, Buxton, Arthur 'stute. Mam a bad head. Brussels taken. Eric home.

13th Sept Fine, filled 12. Shaved. Shelled peas. Football match 2 each. Mam very tired. Tony late in corn. 2 spearheads in Germany.

19th Sept Wet day, filled 9. Paid Ralph 8/4. Found 2 mushrooms. Lord Hartington killed. Mam a bad head. Garage at night, emptied sump. Lads 'stute.

2nd Nov Fine, filled 12. Walked *(with)* Bushie with Eric's bike. Liver and chops, Biddies. Down Petes. Paid Union. Rug pegging. Lads 'stute. Mam very well, a busy day. Fired chimney. 2 bags coal.

30th Jan 1945 Terrible day, ploughs out. Papers came at night. Light failed. Ridded back. Mam fell on steps. Lads went 'stute. Chips for tea. Down Biddies. Russians 95 miles Berlin.

9th May Fine, 2nd V day. Shaved. Home. Leek in afternoon with mam, no market. Hair cut at garage by Ralph. Bonfire on Low at night. No paper. Mam wrote Arthur. Eye a bit easier. Paid motor insurance.

2nd Aug Very hot. Mam wrote Arthur. Filled 12. pick missing, hammer shaft broke. Mam washed. Down Biddies. Legs ache badly. Tony finished hay. 6 clothing coupons.

7th Nov Letter from A. Fine, filled 12. Walked Bushie. Tom Gould home ill. Down Perks and Maggies. Pork pie for tea. Tony, Leek. Mam not too well. Trouble over weighing at work. Haw Haw's appeal dismissed.

27th Nov Arthur went back. Sam Wood killed at Dowlow. Very bad pit, stumps. Filled 10. Cold wind. Walked alone. Emptied radiator. Tony bad cold. Eggs for tea.

[stumps are what's left at the bottom of the working when the face is blown out, which is harder to win than the main blast but has to be cleared out before the next one.]

25th Dec Rained. Letter from A posted aboard HMS Princess Astrid. Card from Alice. Finished *Dangerous Quest*. Tony bought me ale. Finished at dinner. Sleep on couch at night. Mam front room. Mended blackout. Studded shoes.

26th Dec Lovely day, wet night. No post. Shaved. Tony football match, dance at night. Tightened fog lamps and bumper bar. Frank went back. Fire in front room. Fetched milk, 6 eggs. Swept garage out. Miserable.

May 1935.

In Ashwood Dale.

Sunday 26th January 1947 Terrible day, snow, wind and frost. Missed work, in bed till dinner, again in afternoon. Started letter and Littlewoods. Posted papers. Tony bed afternoon. Shippon with Jim at night. Mam never had a rest, knee still improving. Snowplough out. Mutton for dinner. Snake Pass blocked. Foot and mouth Offcote, Ashbourne.

Mon 3rd Feb Seven start. Letter from Arthur, packing goods on train for Pola. Wrote. Littlewoods came. Terrible day, snow, blizzard all day. Ploughs out. Down for bread. Sleep on couch. Mams throat and ears bad. Tony Hindlow *(station)* afternoon. Wilsons abandoned bread van at Thorn. Australia 293 for 4. Tony 'stute at night. Made part of coupon out. Tommy Mycock stranded Dove Holes.

Fri 7th Feb Letter from A. Freezing keener than before. Bus came with snowplough on front, fast at Town End. Ridded up Church Lane. Down Bushies for money, no sweep. Marsh came from Flagg for bread. Bill Skidmore bought our meat. Pie for tea. Fired chimney. Mam cleaned upstairs and front room. Tony 'stute. No coal came. No orders gone to stores.

8th Feb No mail, papers or milk went. All roads blocked, couldn't get Buxton. Down *(village)* Paid for meat and papers. Saw Godfrey in smithy. No motors in Chelly. Out with ploughs. Tony on top in mams bonnet. *(snowridding)* 'stute at night. Mams hands very badly cracked. Still blowing at night, terribly cold.

Sunday 9th Feb Blizzard all day. No motors or papers in Chelly. No milk went. Took Mary Skidmore by van and tractor to meet ambulance. Old Mrs Robinson at Ditch fell, cut her head. Tony and I bed afternoon. Shippon with Jim Mosley at night.*(where they'd sit and talk, warm among the cows)* Started Arthurs letter.

Tues 11th Feb No mail. Roads still blocked. Bagshaw and Whieldon went with tractors for groceries. Down Gilmans first thing. Sent letters and papers to Arthur. Tony on to look at Brough Head stack, Hindlow afternoon. Shaved. 'stute night. Mam washed a little. Still freezing and blowing.

Weds 12th Feb No mail, posted Arthurs letter at Erics. Snowfire *(linament stick)* and Vim. Kirkland came, Jack Wilton here. Biddies for meat. Plane dropped food at Longnor. Mam finished washing. Tony ridding at Shepley. 'stute night. No change forecast, freezing terribly keen. Shaved. Coal getting done. Papers at night. No Leek market.

Thurs 13th Feb 2 letters from Pola, mam wrote. Cleaned upstairs. Still freezing. Buxton with Pete and Eric on Wright's coal motor. Went to coal yard, back on bus to Nook. Cowdale.*(to relations)* Rode with Biddy from Nook. Plane crashed at Grindon, 8 killed. 5 bags coal. Tony ridding on Shepley. Ridded up Church lane. Posted Littlewoods. Called ICI with certificate. Tony 'stute.

Fri 14th Feb No letter, Littlewoods came. Down Biddies for kidney. Inside until night, cold and freezing. Down for bread at night. Lights off all afternoon, street lights cut off at night. Tony ridding to Brough Head stack, 'stute night. Mam finished washing. Sea pie for tea. Stores order not gone again. Miss Button, Staden died.

Sat 15th Feb 2 letters, mam wrote. Posted Alices paper. £2/10/11 from ICI. Paid Biddy. Walked Staden Lane End, picked up by Garlick. Walked all way home. Herrings from Hoopers, Juno Juniper and medicine from Salts. Wireless programmes cut. Mam ironed. Tony bought two cows off Jim. Hay from Brough Head, 'stute at night. Left Union journals at Teddy Tookes. Freezing very keen. Shaved. Left ICI receipt at Holker House.

Sun 16th Feb Terribly keen and cold. Cowdale in morning.(to relations) Rode to Nook with Arthur Longden, walked back, called Bar with 15 coupons. Ridders out in Chelly. Wilsons came with van, backed all way down Church Lane. In Fred Whites over notice from Dowlow. Bed afternoon. Suet balls for dinner. Mams hands very sore.

17th Feb No letter. Still keen and cold. F. White started with snow gang. Tony's cows went. F and M Ashbourne. 2 load hay. Ridded garage, started motor. Up to Thorn to see drift. Down for bread. Posted letter and papers. King and Queen landed Africa. Sundays meat for tea, also pancakes. Mam very tired, hands bad. No sign of better weather.

18th Ridded drift at Thorn, 50 yards from Flagg men.

Sun 23rd Feb Lovely day but very keen. Only one paper. Walked Calton, 6 eggs, round by Common Lane. Ardens taking cows to river to drink. Ridders and plough out. Tony round Pillwill with Woodie.

Both bed afternoon. Shippon with Jim at night. Mam darning. Started letter and Littlewoods. Pools void again. Mam saw moon through window.

26th Isolated again, Tony brought papers at night. No motors in village. Tony on top in afternoon. Thawed slightly. Mam bad head, finished washing. Down smithy afternoon. Carrington and Bramwell digging grave. Mam wrote Arthur at night.

1st March No letter. Fine but terribly keen and cold. Calton early, 6 eggs. Ridded garage, started motor, put chains on. Down for bread, paid Biddy, smithy and rent. Buxton with G Smith, Tony met me back. Receipt, Holker House. German prisoners up Moor Lane. *(ridding)* Tony to Five Wells for 2 cows. Arthurs shoes to Westons.

Weds 5th March Worst blizzard yet, lasted all night and day, everywhere blocked. No mail or papers. Jack came home, blocked with wagon Tideswell Moor all night. Mam finished ironing. Tony on top, 'stute night. Intended signing off. Down Biddies for corn beef. Australia won last test by 5 wickets.

Sunday 9th March Postman walked, 1 old letter from A. lovely day but keen at night and more snow forecast. Ridders at Horsedale. Calton in the morning for potatoes and 6 eggs. Lopped lilac tree, cleaned spouting out, bed afternoon. Tony bed morning and to ridders in afternoon. Shippon with Jim at night. Mam patched trousers ready for work.

11th March 2 postmen walked at night, 5 letters A, 1 Jessie Ogden. Kippers from Alice. Rough morning, filled 26 in pit, home 1.30. Milk went to Bar with Eric. Burnt old shoes. Changed money order. 8 eggs Mavis. Tony sledging hay. 'stute. Freezing again. Hillhead men helped to link up with Bar. Mams chilblains better.

14th March ARTHUR CAME 2.30 in morning, walked from Millers Dale in snow. Filled 3. Ridded garage out. Lads 'stute. Pie for tea. Mams hands very bad. Snowed and freezing keen at night.

20th March Fine, ridded own road, filled 6. Getting wagon up dirt tip afternoon. Up to Thorn. Down to smithy. Got 'Derbyshire Adventure'. Duck for tea. Arthur Dowlow in motor. Tony haycarting. Both lads 'stute. Arthurs £9.10 and gratuity £18.10.6 came by post. 3 bags coal, John Brindley sledging coal as we came from work. Mam tired and hands cracked.

21st Wet day, filled 2, home after dinner. Chicken from Calton. Bushies hand swollen. Buxton afternoon with Arthur. Fish, onions and sausage. Put £48 in post office. Up Church Lane to see jet snow blower. Paid Smith and breadman. Washed overalls. Tony Buxton, haircut. Club money by post. Receipt to Holker House. Posted paper to Alice. Perks gave me petrol coupons.

Sunday 30th March Arthurs last night, feeling sad. Wet day. Mended puncture in morning, bed afternoon, garage at night. Shaved. Mam doing all day. Duck for dinner. Tony bed morning, Flagg afternoon, shippon at night. Arthur Woodward took them to Longnor.

April 1st Snow covered. Filled 11. Mam wrote Arthur. Fresh key from RAC. Sent for petrol. Licenses returned, sent them again. Straightened Arthurs shed and tool box. Mam a quiet and lonely day. 2 bags coal. Finger end easier.

2nd Snowed all day. Letter and Sporting Record from Arthur, posted London. Filled 3, home for dinner. Erics for bread, 12 eggs Mavis, meat Biddies. Shaved. Up garage. Sleep on couch. Mam washed. Tony Leek, 'stute night. John Kidd died. Cheese and onions, pancakes for tea. Stores came for larder. Sent paper Alice.

10th April No letter, mam wrote. Petrol coupons came. Lovely day, filled 12, back not too good. Took meat Mrs Drabble. Pie for tea. Mam indigestion, nap on couch. Tony haycarting. Killed pig at night. 'stute. 2 bags coal. Lot of argument in cabin over 5 day week.

24th No letter, mam wrote. Sent papers to Alice. Fine and windy. Filled 12. 7 on W Redferns road; own road all out, sleepers and rails bent, big hole in end. Posted 2 letters for Calton. Mrs Drabbles money to Biddies. Tony maiden trip on tractor on Shepley with harrows. Mam weary. Paid stores. Bacon and eggs for tea. Ralph Boam home.

26th Heard cuckoo first time.

20th May Up to Thorn with jam jars, found saucepan. *(Thorn pit was the village tip)*

21st June 4 letters Arthur, mam wrote. Timber carrying all morning. Shaved. Back of hand swollen. Buxton with mam. Cowdale turning at night, round Flash Bar and Longnor with mother and Mrs Vaines. 3 gall petrol. Tony putting hay-sweep together. 'stute night. 2nd test match at Lords. Paid Biddy. Valderma for mams eczema

26th June ARTHUR came. Very hot, filled 12. Arthur put switch on iron. New ration books. Paid Mavis. Tony fetched wood for Charlie. Started hay-making. Also at Flatt. Sawed wood. Mended Tony's grass-board. Sent papers to Alice.

3rd July No letter, mam wrote. Filled 11, 2 Brunner. Up to stumps. Took rivets to Calton. Down Biddies for steak. Took ration books. Tony took his to Cliff. Finished sawing wood. Mam ironing. Tony topped stack at night. Hand still swollen. Took saw and trestle back to Moses. *(Grindey)*

10th July Dirty wet day, filled 10. Princess Elizabeth's engagement announced. Len Simpson bought primus cleaners. Wet night. Biddies for steak. Bacon for tea. Tony thistle mowing. Paid Godfrey for saw. Put Longdens license on motor on way home. Mams hands improving.

Sunday 3rd Aug Fine and warm. Indigestion in morning, bed until dinnertime, again with Tone in afternoon. Hay-making at night, finished all but raking. Wrote and posted Arthurs letter and papers, also petrol application. Chapel anniversary. Jelly for supper.

Sunday 10th Aug Clocks put back one hour, dark 9 o'clock. Very hot. Peeled apples and spuds. On couch morning, bed afternoon. Under end watching lads play cricket. Posted paper, started letter. Mam doing well with new teeth.

14th Aug No letter, terribly hot. Mam wrote. White-washed outhouse. Filled 10, 4 Brunners, road wants sleepering. *(stone had to be fresh and broken smaller for the order for Brunner Monds chemical works. Although the men were paid more, it was not a popular job)* Tea at Calton. Sticking with mam at night. Biddy no meat to spare. Tony hacked round corn field, down road at night. No fire in house all day. Puncture in front wheel. Had a talk with Smith at turn.

Sat 16th Aug Hotter than ever. Mended puncture. Sleep on couch, headache. Paid Smith and Skidmore. Buxton with mam. Monyash and Longnor at night. Tony thatching corn stacks. Churchill on wireless.

11th Sept Fine and warm, filled 11, 2 BM. Took shovel to smithy to have shaft fastened. Sawing at night. Swindell started widening Gill Foot entrance. Tony and Arthur Longnor Sports. Down 'stute night. Mams hands still improving. Bottled plums and tomatoes. Washed electric shades. Back not too good.

Sat 15th Nov Letter from A and Littlewoods, mam wrote. Work, filled 6, clocked 11.45. walked Bushie. Black pudding for dinner. Snow, terribly cold wind. Buxton alone. Ink-pen nibs and diary from Pickups, meth from Abbotts. Fynnon Salts. Distilled water from Bar. Tony ploughing. Mams eyes still improving.

Chelmorton, the School. Said to be the Bagshawe boys on the wall.

At the Chelmorton Institute, 1950s.

L to R: Great Grandma,
Aunt Nance and Ma, + Forrester the dog.

BELOW:
Tony Chapman and Gt. Grandad
Chapman with one arm.

Great Gran Chapman,
Grandad & Gran Woodward
Aunt Nance, Norman & Alice.
At Pictor Lodge.

RIGHT:
Mr & Mrs Senior at Chelmorton Post Office.

Chelmorton, near Buxton,

M 191

Payments

To **WM. SMITH, R.S.S.,**
SHOEING & GENERAL SMITH.

**Wheels New Tyred and all kinds of Smiths'
Work done.**

— Five Per Cent. charged on Overdue Accounts. —

1916			
May 26	Journey to have rate signed	7	6
" "	Paid magistrates clerk for signing same	2	.
" "	" " " asper Bill	5	6
July 22	Paid Treasurer union Call	52 .	.
" "	" " R & C. Call	20 .	.
" "	Journey to pay same	7	6
Sep 16	Paid Treasurer union call	50 .	.
" "	" " Special Expenses Call	9 10	.
" "	Journey to pay same	7	6
"	Paid Treasurer R & C call	18 .	.
	Journey returning Jury List	7	6
" 28	Paid Stationer as per Bill	1 6	1
	To Postage Receipt stamps used during half year	. 6	6
	W Smith for services redered as assistant		

George Wheeldon, butcher.

Taking the meat, 1924, Ben Skidmore on right.

CHELMORTON CHAPEL in the early 1960s. A homeless man named Bosley in the 1930s used to get up on top of the porch (centre back in photo) and sleep. Dad said, *'if he was up there when you were in Chapel you could see his boots'.* (AW)

At Flagg, early 1950s. John Goodwin, David Mycock, Maurice Goodwin, Sheila & Maureen Boam.

At 3 Rock Cottages, Flagg. The Goodwin boys and friend.

At Lane Farm, Newtown.

Peter Mellor

Mrs Bagshawe, Fred's wife from Brierlow Bar, used to be a nurse and she brought me into the world at Netherlow, Chelmorton. My father, Solomon, did the snow ploughing; Mr Raines used to help him, they supplied two horses each. They went to Brierlow Bar and Heathfield Nook and the other way to the RAC box on the A6 near Taddington. There was a plank in between the sides of the plough which could be fixed in 3 places and they had it narrow when they went and wider when they came back. I remember as a little lad standing with the horses while they went in the house to have a drink. That day it was wet underneath the snow as the horses sloshed through it, eighteen inches to two feet deep.

Mr Raines built a slaughterhouse at Town End and bought a butchers van and delivered meat. I was once knocked down on the road and was in hospital unconscious. When I was ready to come home, Mr Raines fetched me home in the butchers van. Another time Bob Woods who worked for him was fetching the cows one evening from up the field and fell in a rut. I was looking as he lay there; I thought it was a dead sheep. He'd got a broken leg and they came with the butchers van and a board and took him; it was like an ambulance.

1930s. Back: Harold Mellor, Teddy Dawson
Front: Peter & Harry Mellor

In wartime we had a brown duck which was badly; it couldn't walk. My brother, Harold picked it up, turned it upside down and he could feel there was an egg crossways on, so he pressed on her body to turn it and I caught three eggs; she was egg-bound. That was a bonus with rationing being on.

One day we were going to school about quarter to nine and we heard all this noise coming and there were two elephants walking side by side and a man on a piebald horse with a big whip behind. Most of us got over the wall; we were frightened because of the noise they made when he cracked the whip. They threw their trunks up and trumpeted, I don't know if their feet were sore. One of them stopped and left a massive pile of droppings and later dad loaded it onto a cart and he always said where he'd put it in the field - the elephant muck! They must have come from Bakewell, setting off at four in the morning to come over Sheldon Moor on the way to Buxton.

I've worked on all the farms in the Chelmorton area at one time or another, harvesting, potato picking, hay making. We came to this farm, the Organ Ground at Monyash in 1966, Mr Wakefield, the Army Stores man wanted to buy a farm and wanted a tenant; so I put my name down and got it. I've heard several stories of how it got its name; one that they sold the land to buy an organ for Bakewell Church; another that gypsies used to camp here and play organs, and another is that the land was sold and the proceeds were used to build the Sunday School at the back of the chapel in Monyash. We have since bought the farm.

George Wheeldon, a butcher at Chelmorton, when he was going out left Sam Wilton, who worked for him, a long list of jobs to be done. Sam looked through the list, stroking his chin and

Back: Marion Jones, Bunty Hill, Margaret Lomas, Betty Hodgkinson, Mary Sharpe, Margaret Wheeldon.
Middle: Jean Robinson, Harry Mellor, George Grooby, Sidney Bagshaw, Derek Mycock, Les Smith, Isobel Dicken.
Front: Peter Mellor, Brian Wilton. Early 1940s. Teacher at back, Miss 'Burdican'.

asked, *'What about the snow ridding?'* George snapped back, *'There's no snow ridding, what're you talking about?'* Sam said, *'There will be by the time I've done all these jobs!'*

Nattie Arden owned the Bull i'th'Thorn and Ben Handley used go up cleaning the pigs out on the farm. There was a slaughterhouse there, where the function room is - that's where they used kill the pigs. Ben asked what about his wages. Nat replied, *'Ow many meals 'ast 'ad?'* Ben told him so Nattie then said, *'Oh, they't well paid then!'* They called him Nattie because they said he could skin a gnat!

Nattie had a race from Ashbourne with horse and trap to Buxton. He was winning till he got to Bull i'th'Thorn when the horse stopped - it thought it was home.

Chelmorton School, 1950s.

Main Street, Chelmorton. My father, Solomon Mellor, making the pavement.

Monyash.

Old Market Cross and Village Square, Monyash.

Church Lane, Chelmorton.

Church Lane, Chelmorton.

Maurice Goodwin

I was born at Monyash, father was a farm labourer. We moved to Snitterton near Matlock for a while then to Wheal Farm at Flagg. I went to Flagg school and every dinner time they used to take most of the children to the Institute at Chelmorton for our dinners; 2 taxi loads. Bagshawes from Brierlow Bar took us. It was exiting because there weren't many cars about. I always used to sit in the front and change gear for him; I used to watch what his leg was doing and when he pressed the clutch, flirt the gearstick through. They were big black old Wolsley cars; we thought we were royalty; 8 or 9 kids crammed in each car.

Mr Frank Moores owned the Wheal Farm and dad lived there and looked after his stock and kept a few of his own as well. He also worked for Sanders Garage on Spring Gardens in Buxton. They had coaches and he used to wash and service them.

Peeling the spuds, Maurice & John.

I once remember my brother had had a good hiding because he'd been a naughty lad; mum had give him a bit o' lace round his legs and he run off and went missing, we couldn't find him. Me mother and meself, we were proddlin' in the mere holes and tanks with sticks, we thought he'd fell in one and drowned. Dad came home from work and was searchin'. We went into the implement shed, where there was a big hay loader. They used to have a rack on top which could tip down to load onto the carts and he was lain hidden on top o'that out of the way.

The water was saved off the roof into a tank at the back of the house, everything had to be boiled. Sam Wilton used come down Flagg on an old Standard Fordson, like hell out of gear, stood up, fag in his mouth all blowin' up, to fetch water from the stand tap at the bottom of the village. And comin' back up, smoke flyin' out of exhaust and Sam still with fag on and tank full of water on back to Bosley Fields.

My granny Prince at Lane Farm, Newtown used to carry water to the cows from troughs down the lane quarter of a mile away with yokes. 64 years they were there, rented from the Harpur Crewes.

When Sanders packed up, Kennings took the garage over; it was Austin/Rover then. Dad went lime-drawing at Ryan and Somervilles at Hindlow; he biked there. I always remember him telling me that he went one morning, it was raining very hard and he was three minutes late. Old Ryan was sit at clock box watchin' 'em all in and he sent dad home; he was saturated.

One year, I remember the walls in Flagg were level with snow and 5 or 6 men walked to Buxton in a blizzard to fetch bread and paraffin. Dad, Harold Bosley, Frank Brough, Rafe Boam and Jud Boam. And I remember wakening one mornin' and somethin' were scratchin' on the front o' me pyjamas in bed. I threw the clothes off to get up and there were a mouse in bed with me

Colin Goodwin at Meadow House, Chelmorton.

DERBYSHIRE COUNTY COUNCIL 20584
EDUCATION COMMITTEE

MR. W. N. HANDLEY,
FOR TRUSTEES WAR MEMORIAL INST.
WAR MEMORIAL INSTITUTE,
CHELMORTON,
BUXTON, DERBYS.

Chelmorton C. SCHOOL

TO RENT OF PREMISES/LAND FOR
MONTH
QUARTER ENDED
HALF YEAR
YEAR _____ 24th September, 1955.

AT _____ War Memorial Institute.

FOR _____ School Canteen.

1 WEEKS @ 2/6 per week			2	6
3 WEEKS @ 18/6 per week	2	15	6	
£	2	18	-	

Authorised for Payment	Calculations Checked		
Creditor			
Code		Amount	

Charlie Prince (Grandad) at Lane Farm, Newtown.

and up t' the bedroom winder was a drift o' snow. I goes downstairs, opens door, it was one solid block o' snow, yer couldn't get out. So I shut it quick before it caved in; we had t' get out at the back door. The toilet was out the back and yer had t' rid t' get there.

Fred Redfern was the knackerman at Flagg and we used go round with him sometimes. *'I'm going such and such to pick a horse up; are you coming?'* It was interesting to go with him in his old cattle wagon, there weren't many about. I've been all over the place with him fetchin' horses and cows in. We went up Flash and the dead horse was down a field, they had drag it up

Maurice & John with Grandma, Sarah Prince, at Wheal Farm, 1950.

with tractor. When we got back to the knacker yard it was dark; he said, *'Go and switch that light on.'* And when I did, there were that many rats-there was a block out o' the wall and there were that many tryin' get through this hole, they were jammed. I was about ten. Years ago, dad used to say he'd seen 'em movin' in droves, hundreds on Flagg Moor.

Old Walter Redfern was a rum feller. At night, he used throw an owd rug down in front o' t' fire and chew twist and spit on this rug ow night, then roll it up and shove it in corner till next night.

I remember the crates full o' bombs stacked on Sheldon Moor by the roadside, stacked ever so high. It was known as Bomb Lane - they seemed to be stacked everywhere.

Flagg School, 1950s.
Back: Barry Williams, Phillip Goodwin, Maurice Lomas, Maurice Boam.
2nd: Paul Bisgrove, Wilf Jones, Joyce Findlow, Gwen Naylor, Joyce Boam, Geoff Lomas, Roger Dicken.
3rd: Maureen Williams, Stella Boam, Margaret Redfern, Carol Heathcote, Joan White, Jacqueline Breeze, Neville Boam.
David Mycock, Maurice Goodwin, John Goodwin, Tommy & Patrick Rogers, Duggie Bolton.

Charlie Boam

There were 11 of us; I was born in 1915 at Sycamore Farm, Taddington. We moved up to Moorgrange and had to walk the 2 miles to Priestcliffe School every day. I used to go to my aunty Annie Beswicks at Five Wells to stay.

Dad used to send me off with the horse to take to the smithy at Chelmorton. He'd give me a leg up and I used to take it. We moved to Wheal farm when I was 11.

Eva and Maurice Boam at Ash Tree Farm, Flagg, 1950s.

When I started work, I never had a penny till I was 19; dad took it all off me for my keep. I had £25 a year for working at Sam Swindell's farm at Chelmorton.

Albert Redfern was the knacker, he only had one arm, the other had a hook on. He could shoot; he'd be up early and owd Tagg *(Hodgkinson)* used follow him with a dog and if he shot a hare, the dog would pick it up and take it back to Tagg. Albert threatened shoot it if it got close enough. He knew where the hares were and when the hunt turned out at Flagg, he'd show them where one lay and they'd give him 10s. This day, he'd got a hare in the field across from Flagg Hall, he'd been watching it. When they turned up, they wouldn't give him the money so he fetched his gun and shot it.

Maurice and Neville Boam at Ash Tree Farm, Flagg, 1950.

At Flagg Races.

At Hubberdale, Flagg.
We think these are Miss Howe, Miss Rose Mellor, Aunt Alice Mellor, Mrs Howe.

Flagg water supply, the Well Yard 1910.
Photos courtesy of Mrs B. Wilkson.

Billy Allen, the pump driver, starting the engine.

Mr John Willie Howe from Hardy Barn, with Mrs Howe, daughter Ivy and grandaughter Joyce.
At Hubberdale Farm.

1923 at Moor Grange.
Mr & Mrs Ernest Boam with Joe, Ernest, Charlie, Herbert, Mary, Jack and Frank.

Ernie Boam

I was born in 1914. On the 5th November in Flagg all the lads in the village used to go raiding people's farmyards and pinch the carts, milk floats, gates, all sorts and put them in the 'Doms' in front of John Willie Naylors. That was the watering place for Naylor's cows and George Allen's at Highfields and Jack Wain at Dalehead. In wintertime they had to cut holes in the ice and we used to go sliding on it on the way to school. There were about 28 of us lads; every farmer kept two lads then. The next morning they were sent to fetch every thing back.

I've attended Flagg Chapel most of my life. We had a good choir, a dozen or so. On Good Friday we had a Service of Song; it would be packed full. Percy Rains of Chelmorton preached now and then - we had to put screens in the Sunday school to get people in, the same at harvest.

We had Sunday School outings by horse and trap to Rudyard Lake or Ilam. There'd be 6 or 7 traps, load all the children up and get off to Ilam Hall; have tea then go down Dovedale, across the stepping stones, have another tea and then come back. It was lovely - something different.

There was a party at Christmas and on Christmas Eve we'd have a do at chapel then about 11 o'clock at night about 20 of us would set off and go round carol singing; it could be 4am when we got in. We'd set off up the village, do the two farms at the back of 'the Hills', then down Flagg Lane, up to the Wheal, down Monyash Dale to Mountney's and over the hill to Knotlow Farm. Going through Mountney's fields we used to get a little turnip to eat. Then back to Flagg and down the village, finishing at John Willie Naylors. He always had the kettle on, even in the middle of the night. We had a cup of tea there and then went home.

The next morning when I'd milked and had my breakfast, I went round again to collect the money for the chapel. By the time I got home I was sozzled; I'd land back about 6 when they were milking; I usually missed my Christmas dinner.

Bill Wood from Knotlow used come chapel and his wife would come down after with the storm lamp in her hand. Always about 10 minutes after. She walked back home in front of him, he often stopped in Flagg for a while, talking.

Old John Dicken from up Flagg Moor, he used get 'blue uns' and get the gun out; the wife used run to Flagg and other folks had to go up and sober him down before she'd go back to him.

Jockey Jack Needham used to sit at the side of the road breaking stone all day. He had a round nappin' hammer. There were a lot of little fields and they took some of the walls out between Flagg and Taddington to make them bigger. It was tipped at the side of the road and Jack used to break it. Then he'd level it up and make a big heap of it and be paid so much a square yard and that made Jarnet from Taddington to Flagg and to Chelmorton over the top.

Jack Wain and his sister Emma lived at Dalehead Farm at the bottom o' Flagg. Owd Jack used milk at night with lad and Emma and lad milked in a morning. Lad used take the cows up to Doms for a drink then walk 'em and tent 'em right to top o' Jarnet, come back, have his dinner, clean the sheds out, then go back and fetch 'em for milkin'. Ow summer that was, a little 4 acre field with a mere in it; they'd milk 18 or 20. Th' owd lad, when he died, they couldna get him down stairs, they had t' get him out of a bedroom winder; he was a big feller.

Harry Wilkson farmed at Ivy Farm, Herbert and William Lomas and a lad at Flagg Hall, John Willie Naylor and two sons at Hobson Farm, George Allen with a family of 11 at Highfield - 7 sons and 4 daughters, feeding pigs and keeping hens-bringing 'em all up. Albert Redfern had 9 - there were no allowances then. All of them went to Flagg school.

I went to Flagg Races in 1920s; Doris Allen at Back of Hill worked for mother at Moorgrange and on race day she brought me, Joe and Charlie down here to Flagg and up to the races. I remember the Prince of Wales (Duke of Windsor) coming - he had two horses and rode in one race but fell off second time round at the back of Mark Dicken's. 1929 that was. Sometimes he came to hunt; people were thrilled to bits to see royalty up there.

Billy Allen used live at top of Flagg. In the 1930s, I worked with him repairing clay meres. We started in the bottom and cleaned it out, then took the stone pitchings out for about a yard up all round from the bottom. Then we cleaned the fine ashes off which had been put on to stop the stones from going through the clay. Then we dug the clay off and took it to the top to clean it; there was lime stuck on it, you had a trowel and wiped it off. Underneath was lime ashes to stop the worms from coming up. We put wet bags on the clay to keep it soft. Then we used to start again in the bottom; put the lime ashes down, put the clay back and work it, beat it together 4 to 6 inches thick, fit the stone on and then get limestone dust from Dowlow to fill the nicks up round the stones and then when it rained and there was some water in the bottom, you could start higher up and take another layer around and do the same again until you got to the top. If there was water in the bottom you could keep wetting the bags to keep the clay soft. We were paid £1 per yard diameter of the mere. When we were going to school we used to drink water out of the meres - get down and sup it; not where the cows were, but a nice clean mere in a field.

We were very keen on cricket; there were 7 of us brothers playing for Flagg at one time. We won the Buxton and District League seven times between 1934 and 1952. All the village turned out when we were playing and if we went to Buxton, they'd all go with us. I think cricket came before farming Saturday afternoon and Wednesday night; they did the milking when they got back. We played in the field next to the school. At the end of the season there was a big do. There were 16 teams in the league; postmen, Co-op, LMS, doctors, Chelmorton, Flagg, Pomeroy, Peak Forest, Peak Dale, Burbage, Ladmanlow... we finished up at the White Lion on Spring Gardens; there was supper and presentation of medals and the Sir Alfred Law Shield.

It was a marvellous thing; there's no life in the village now-if it weren't for the chapel, we'd have nothing; we haven't even got a pub now. In 1975 they closed the school, though we fought hard to keep it open.

Buxton Park 1952. All Boams - Frank, Ernest, Stanley. Front: Charlie with Derek, Harry and Herbert.

Wendy Fearn

I came to Pictor Hall in March 1963 when father bought the farm. While I've been farming here, I've been very interested in finding out some of the history of the area.

There was an ancient settlement here dating back to the 14th century and known as Pigtor or Pigtorre. It was probably a hamlet until the late 1700s when the 'new' hall was built . I think it would have faced the other way to where the drive comes down through a beautiful area planted with trees as a park around 1800.

There are the remains of a tower at the front of the garden which I understand was where the ladies could see the progress of the hunt with views down into Ashwood Dale. It would have been a busy place - there is a bell mounted on the barn which was used to summon the men for meals, 15 at one time. There is a range of stables built in the late 1800s where shire horses were bred and trained and went for the cavalry.

We have two lodges, one in Ashwood Dale which my late friend Dr Joyce Critchlow told me dates back to 1450. The other, Tym Lodge is where Thomas Tym and his family lived in 1800. In 1820 the hall was burgled and valuables were supposed to have been hidden in Deepdale. They were never recovered.

At Redgap, up the lane, there is a barn near the house which Thomas Daykin of Bailey Flatt allowed people to use as a church in the time of Queen Mary when there was religious persecution. When the barn was made into a cowshed and concrete was laid on the floor some years ago, I was told they covered up stone slabs on the floor with peoples names carved on them.

The lane from there down to Woo Dale is known as Church Lane and there were supposed to have been burials down the side of it.

Further along Redgap lane, across the field are the remains of Dale Head which was also a shire stud. Mr Bradbury who had lived there told me there were several studs and some jiggery pokery was going on and there was a stable made underground-the entrance was concealed, but he had never found it. It may just have been a tall story.

By MESSRS. HAMPSON BROS.,

At the "CHESHIRE CHEESE," BUXTON,

ON

Thursday, the 1st day of August, 1912,

AT 6 O'CLOCK IN THE EVENING PRECISELY,

Subject to conditions of sale (including the Common Form Conditions of the Buxton Law Society) to be then produced.

Both the above mentioned residences are most excellently and romantically situated commanding extensive and picturesque views typical of the Peak District, and are in first rate repair and condition. There is convenient access to the Buxton and Bakewell main road over private bridges.

The land is in good heart and the offer affords an opportunity rarely to be met of acquiring property eminently suitable for a stud farm for the breeding and rearing of horses or cattle or for sporting purposes. The property at Deep Dale has been let as a shooting box, and is very suitable for that purpose.

There is on the land at Pictor and Woolow a very valuable bed of limestone (for which Buxton and its neighbourhood are celebrated), and as the properties adjoin the Midland Railway and there is a face of limestone at least 150 feet in height above the level of the Railway, it will be at once seen that here is a chance which cannot recur of obtaining a property admirably adapted for the production of lime in large quantities.

Norman Beswick

On our farm, here at Daisymere, we have six fields which we refer to as Sally's fields. I think it would have been a smallholding, Sally Goodwin lived over there in a wood, I just remember the remains of a fireplace, there is just a decaying barn there now. Next to it is Dale Head, which Mr Whitehead had as a shire stud. It was still a proper farm in my time; there were shippons and the Bradburys sent milk and all the lot, then it got into a bad way and ICI knocked it down. The building that's left was originally the saddle room to the stud. It was boarded round inside where they hung all the harness and there was a fireplace. Bradburys used it as a house when they were there. There were stories of ghostly noises which was also said to be horses in the underground stables, but I think it was codswallop.

RIGHT: Walter Salt, Breeze Mount Farm, Waterswallows, at Bakewell market 1970

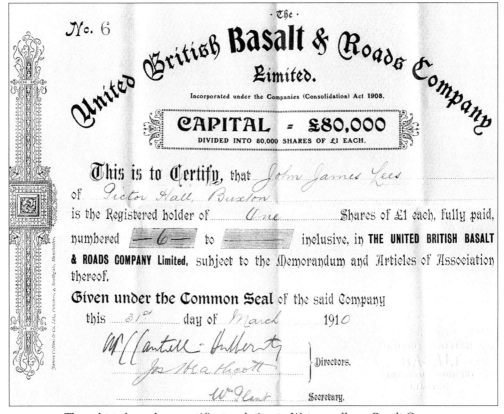

Thought to be a share certificate relating to Waterswallows Basalt Quarry.

Opening of Waterswallows Quarry, 1910. Samuel Swann Brittain far right.

Salt's cows passing Waterswallows plant - Hughes Brothers
- showing the aggregate bins and Tarmac plant. 1960.

Dale Head with the mere in the foreground.
Demolished April 2008.

Christine Gregory

I've helped with a lot of rag rugs when I was at home as a girl. That was in the days before television, though we did have radio of course. My mum, Annie Higginbottom was always making rag rugs and I used to be cutting up and helping to put the patterns on. They were on old sugar bags; that was because she came from New Mills and her aunt had a little shop down Torr Top street. Torr Top has nearly all gone now, made into a huge car park; but Aunty Sarah's house still stands; it was number 21 and had a shop front. Every time I go to New Mills now, I go to have a look, it's still a shop to me, but obviously it's a house now.

The people who lived down Torr Top were not very well off, but she kept them going. They had a weekly bill and sometimes at the end of the week they couldn't pay it, so she just carried it over to the next one and when she died there were a lot of people in New Mills owed her a lot of money, because they had been moved away from Torr Top onto a new housing estate in a different part of New Mills and they just left their debts behind them and forgot about them.

We lived at Sparrowpit and I can remember my mother went down to the shop two days a week to help, so on a Saturday, when I wasn't at school, we were down there for about half past eight in the morning ready for the shop to open and I used to sit at the back bagging sugar into pounds and half-pounds into little blue bags with a little scoop. Then I had to bang them on the table and there was a special way of folding them in. Aunty Sarah was only four foot nothing; she wore clogs with metal runners on, on the bare flag floors which were skittered with sand; I shall never forget the sound, it went through me. She was very particular when you were bagging the sugar; it didn't have to be a half ounce over or a half ounce under.

The bags the sugar came in were very closely woven, so mother used to bring them home and wash them, then undo the stitching and sew two together, so we had very big rag rugs. She'd picked up from jumble sales dark coloured woollen clothes, which she washed first, so it looked like Casey's Court at our house with sacks hanging out and old clothes, all dark coloured. Then I helped draw the patterns on and we would decide which colour was going where; then it would be rag rugging, especially wet days and at nights. I didn't enjoy it very much.

The Farming Life Centre rag rug which I made recently is made from an old army blanket; I don't know whether it's from the First or Second world war. That was from here, from Blackwell, from the house. The natural colour on the rug is from an old felt which came off the rollers at the old bleach works down at the Strines at New Mills, my grandfather, Eli Higginbottom was one of the foremen down there. When they renewed them, they had to take them off these huge rollers; I never saw it, it was what my mother told me. They would give them to the worker to take home. They'd all got large families. They washed them, cut them up and made them into blankets for the beds. When my mum died 12 years ago, she still had felt on her bed at Sparrowpit and this is it. It has been up in our attic ever since. So when I was looking for something to use, I thought that will go with the brown of the old army blanket.

But I've often thought of my grandma washing them because they were huge things, the one that I've got would easily fit a king-size bed now. They would all be feather beds in those days. They used to have one underneath between the springs and the mattress and use the others on the top. But the thoughts of washing them after coming from the bleach works, they'd be covered in bleach; they would cut them up into sizes, then wash them with a posser in a dolly tub, then put them through the wooden rollers of the mangle, then hang them out to dry. It must be close to 100 years old, because Grandad died in 1941 and retired a good time before.

They had ten children and my grandad was what you would call an alcoholic now, but they didn't then. They had to have something in those days because they didn't lead very nice lives, it was all work. So mum was one of ten; she also had two brothers who died after having the vaccine. One was about one month and one four months old. Ever after that, my grandma wouldn't have any more vaccinated. It would be the smallpox vaccine.

Days were different then, very hard in the mills. Though some of them didn't work at all. No money and no jobs. The children down there, about my age then, it sounds terrible but they didn't have knickers on or those sort of things. If they had got a dress on they were lucky. Some of them didn't have anything on their feet.

Aunty Sarah sold everything in the shop. In one side of the shop there were second hand clothes hung up, old shirts and teeth, anybody that died, they took their false teeth out, she'd a big drawer full of them. People would come in and say, *'I've broke me false teeth, Sarah, have you got any to sell?'* And a drawer full of glasses; if your eyesight started to fail, you went to see Sarah Jane and she'd fit you up with a pair of glasses. You tried them on until you found a pair that you could see better through.

She was an amazing woman, Aunty Sarah. Her family, the Princes, originated from Parwich. There were six children, my grandma was another one and their father, he also drank. He was out one night shooting rabbits. He had a horse and trap and he used to stand up and shoot from it; probably that was the only meat they had. They were so poor, I can remember Aunty Sarah telling me that at this little cottage in Parwich, near to the church, where they lived, *'We used to climb out of the back bedroom window and there was a lean-to underneath it; we used to slide down the roof, then go up the back garden and dig up a potato or turnip and eat it in the middle of the night, we were so hungry.'*

The old man hit a stone and came out of the trap and broke his neck while shooting, so their mother was left with six children and no money. She used to take in washing, then a local man came along and thought he would take her on with all these children. Then she started another family of course and I think another four children came along.

They went out to service; my grandma, Annie went into service, she'd be thirteen; she worked at a big house. She earned £1 a year and had to pay for any breakages and she was heavy-handed all her life and I think at the end of the year she owed them more than they owed her.

Aunty Sarah, she never married; she came down to New Mills to live with her aunt who had the little shop. She was a spinster, Miss Louisa Marsh and when she died, Sarah took over and remained a spinster all her life. She was full of love and goodness, she never saw any harm in anyone, she'd help anybody. I thought she was lovely.

She had these lovely little brass scales, very, very delicate. They fascinated me, and when she wasn't in the shop I used to be putting the little weights on and if she could hear it, she'd shout *'Are you playin' with them scales?'* And I'd say, *'No.'* She said to me one day, *'You shall 'ave 'em when I've gone.'* And I have, I've still got them. They were purely for tobacco and in the drawer below, there were big coils of twist, horrible stuff and St. Bruno, which smelt absolutely divine. She had a big damp cloth on top to keep it moist so that it would weigh well.

She sold every food you could think of and sweets, a big row of them; but she didn't call them sweets, she called them spits. And whenever I was leaving with mother, she would say, *'Take a few spits with you.'* And gave me a few in a paper bag to take home to Sparrowpit with me. That was wartime, everything was rationed, but she always managed a few spits.

They had another sister, Martha Prince; she worked on farms in the Ashborne area when she was a girl. She was working where they had Ayrshire cows with huge horns. She was milking by hand and one whipped round and caught its horn in her mouth and ripped her face right up and it was just stitched together rough and it made a real mess of her. She never married. She ended up working for a wealthy family at Whaley Bridge; until she was too old to work.

Down at Aunty Sarah's, the toilets were way down the back, a long way away. There were rows and rows of houses and they used to share, four or five to a toilet. They were immaculately clean. I've never seen or heard of any toilets like them since. What they were was a big round earthenware pipe, which was quite high really; I had a job to sit on it. It had a white wooden scrubbed seat which was very clean and you could hear water running all the time and apparently what it was somewhere down below was a pan with water running constantly into it, which when it was full, it tipped and came back to level again. I didn't know this, I thought it was just a hole going down to eternity with a river in the bottom. My sister, Pauline is nine years younger than me and when she must go to the toilet when we were at Aunty Sarah's, I had to take her and I was terrified that she was going to fall down this hole and I'd never see her again. So I used to hang on to her for dear life while she was sat on the front of this toilet with the water running down the back.

Grandma & Aunty Sarah.

Aunty Sarah had lovely little yellow canaries and they used to sing their little hearts out in their two little cages. I can remember when one of them died, Pauline and me went and buried it down near these toilets and had a little service and sang a hymn and put a little cross up. Aunty Sarah kept them going for years; she used to give them a drop of brandy if they looked a bit poorly and she gave them a little bath in two tiny blue dishes every Saturday morning when we were there with a bit of warm water. It had to be a certain temperature. Put it in for them to have their bath, then take it away again and empty it and do it again on the next Saturday. So I've not only got the brass scales, but the blue dishes as well.

But eventually both canaries died and she decided she wouldn't replace them, she did love them. She lived on her own for many years but eventually my grandma, who'd had the ten children moved out of St Marys road and went to live with Aunty Sarah; so two sisters lived together. Grandma did all the baking and Sarah ran the shop until she was a very old lady. And the youngest son, who took over grandma's house, was in the Airborne Division and dropped at Arnhem; we've still got his red beret.

The backing on the rug is one of Aunty Sarah's bolster covers from her bed, made of twill. I was looking round, thinking, *'What can I back it with?'* and in this cupboard, I found Aunty Sarah's bolster case; I thought, *'That'll do.'* So she'll be remembered in the Farming Life Centre.

Occasionally, in my school holidays, I'd go down and stay with Aunty Sarah and grandma for a week perhaps. Always on a Sunday, we didn't open the shop, we went to chapel. Aunty Sarah was a Sunday school teacher as well at the 'Prims.' And after the service, in the afternoon she'd say *'Come on, we'll go for a ride.'* And we'd get on a bus and I can remember once she took me to Lyme Park; but we had to get off this bus when we were only half way home. I said, *'Why have we got off here?'* She said, *'I want to show you this garden.'* So we walked up between these houses and she said, *'What do you think about that?'* It was all gnomes. She thought it was wonderful; I thought it was awful but I said it was lovely. Then we walked back down the road, caught the next bus and went home.

In blackberrying time, we went every night down to Strines; that was in the late forties; we used to love it. When my mother was a girl, aged nine or ten, she was born in 1908, she used to take her dad's dinner down every day to the works. While she was down there, they used to give her all these bets and she used to run up back into New Mills and put these bets on. So all her life, she was always looking at the newspaper and she'd say, *'That one'll win,'* or *'This one'll win.'* She never bet, but she knew about horses and things.

She learnt to play the piano and when the man who played at the cinema in New Mills was poorly, she used to play for the silent movies, so she was quite good at improvising. She never actually went out to work, she was the eldest girl of these ten children and she was busy along with her mother looking after all these babies. She always said she brought the youngest one up. She also learned hairdressing, so cut all their hair.

Grandma was a big knitter, knitting socks all the time. She knit socks and turned heels without looking; she did them with double heels so that when the first layer wore out, you nicked a bit of wool, pulled it out and there was a new one underneath. Because they had all these boys, two of the older ones went over to relatives in Canada to live with them; they hadn't got any children. They were supposed to stay but I think they only did two years and came back. Grandma was most upset because she'd fitted them up with about six pairs of stockings and when they came back, they'd worn them the right way, worn the second heels out, then turned them over the other way as well with the heels on top.

They went to live with this uncle and his wife, they were very mean and eking out a living in the forests in Canada and were extremely rough. They always told a tale that this uncle chopped all his toes off with an axe when they were working out in the woods; but he never stopped work, just carried on until they got back at night and then they took his boots off and sock with his toes inside. Breakfast was a bucketful of hen's eggs put on the fire to boil and then they just put the bucket in the middle of the table and they had to help themselves.

My dad, Frank Fletcher worked on the farm at Sparrowpit for granddad, Francis Fletcher; only a small farm on Rushup Edge, so he and his brother Sam went to work in the quarries, filling and breaking stone. Then in the 30s he went to work at Eldon Hill as a lorry driver, till about 1949 and then he became a foreman in the garage, So when my mum and me were going down to New Mills, all the lorry drivers knew her and would stop and pick us up and drop us at the Swan and we'd walk down into New Mills. Sometimes they'd drop us off a bit earlier than the Swan; that's on the main road to Stockport and we'd drop down and walk at the side of the canal. One day mum said, *'This is what we used to do when we were girls; we used to walk on these stones on the edge.'* And she slipped and nearly fell in. I didn't realise at the time, mother was pregnant with my sister; I just thought she had a big blue coat on. We never did that again.

We used to walk from there down past Swizzells sweet works; I used to think it was heaven walking past there, the smell! Going over one of the bridges, we always had to stop and look over at the barges on the canal down below, all filling up with bottles; the beginning of recycling you see. The bottles used to come down a big chute into these barges and then away they'd go to the emery paper works.

Third Edition—Revised to July 28th, 1917.

FOOD REGULATIONS.

Summary of Orders which apply to the Public.

*** *Copies of this Summary may be obtained post free from the Publicity Bureau, Ministry of Food, Grosvenor House, W. 1. Details will be found in the Orders themselves, the titles and numbers of which are given at the end of each section. The Orders referred to may be obtained from any bookseller at the price of 1d. or direct from H.M. Stationery Office, Kingsway, W.C. 2, post free 1½d.*

The following is a summary of the Orders issued by the Food Controller from time to time and now in force. Only those provisions are given which are of general interest, and they are arranged under the headings of subjects and not of the Orders as made.

BARLEY AND BREWING.

The Food Controller has taken over all barley, foreign and home-grown, other than home-grown barley which has not been kiln-dried.

By an Order made in March the output of beer in each quarter was limited to one-third of the output during the corresponding quarter of the year, 1st April, 1915, to 31st March, 1916.

By a further Order made in July the barrelage during the quarter commencing 1st July, 1917, was increased by 20%, provided that any brewer accepting this increase brews one-half of his total output at a gravity not exceeding an original gravity of 10368. The remaining half shall be brewed at an average original gravity not exceeding that of the total brewed by him during the quarter commencing July 1st, 1916.

A further increase of barrelage not exceeding 13 1/3% may be authorised by licence of the Food Controller and will be allocated to such munition and agricultural areas as are found still to be deficient in supplies.

Brewers who do not elect to come under the Order are not affected.

The manufacture and sale of malt is prohibited, except under licence.

Barley and its products, in common with oats and maize, may not be used except under licence for any purpose other than seed, human and animal food, or in the manufacture of articles of food other than glucose.

[*Barley (Requisition) Order, 1917, No. 364 ; Maize, Barley and Oats (Restriction) Order, 1917, No. 404 ; Brewers (Malt Purchases) Order, 1917, No. 132 ; Malt (Restriction) Order, 1917, No. 159 ; Intoxicating Liquor (Output and Delivery) Order, 1917, No. 270 ; Ditto. No. 2, No. 700 ; Malt (Restriction) Order, 1917, No. 345.*]

BEANS, PEAS AND PULSE.

All imported beans, peas and pulse have been taken over by the Ministry of Food.

The following maximum retail prices have been fixed:— Large butter beans, 10d. per lb. until June 30th, 9d. during July, and 8d. thereafter ; white haricot beans, for the same periods, 8d., 7d. and 6d. ; coloured haricot beans, 7½d., 6½d. and 5½d. ; blue and green peas (whole and split), 9d., 9d. and 9d. ; large manufactured lentils, 8d., 8d. and 8d. ; small manufactured lentils, 7d., 7d. and 7d. ; yellow split peas, 6d., 6d. and 6d.

All must be sold by weight only, and may be used only for human consumption.

Until August 15th, beans, peas and pulse, packed before May 30th, m..y be sold in the package at prices exceeding those permitted by the above Order. The onus of proving that the article was so packed rests upon the seller in the case of proceedings.

The use before December 1st of winter sown Winter Beans grown in the United Kingdom in the year 1917 is forbidden for any purpose other than seed. No such beans may be bought or sold to any person other than such persons as ordinarily deal in them and with a view to their being used or re-sold for the purposes of seed. In cases of purchase the buyer must give a certificate to the seller giving the name and address of the buyer and stating the purpose for which such beans are required. This certificate must be retained by the seller and be open to the inspection of any authorised person. The Order does not refer to Ireland.

[*Beans, Peas and Pulse (Requisition) Order, 1917, No. 457 ; Beans, Peas and Pulse (Retail Prices) Order, 1917, No. 511 ; Winter Beans Order, 1917, No. 766.*]

BREAD AND CEREALS.

Bread must not be sold until it has been made at least 12 hours.

The only loaves allowed are the tin loaf, the one-piece oven-bottom loaf, pan Coburg shape, and twin sister brick loaves, and rolls weighing not less than 1 oz. and not more than 2 ozs.

No currant, sultana, or milk bread may be made.

No sugar may be used in bread.

All bread must be sold by weight. All loaves must be 1 lb. or an even number of pounds.

No wheat, rye, rice, tapioca, sago, manioc, or arrowroot or products thereof may be used except for human food.

No wheat, rye, rice, no flour thereof, nor any article containing such flour, shall be damaged or wasted.

No maize, barley, or oats, or products thereof may be used except for seed or human or animal food.

The maximum price of home-grown wheat is fixed at 78/- per quarter of 480 lbs. ; of home-grown barley (other than kiln-dried) at 65/- per quarter of 400 lbs. ; and of home-grown oats at 55/- per quarter of 312 lbs. Damaged home-grown grain may not be sold at a higher price than the above.

The extraction of flour from wheat is raised to a nominal basis of 81 per cent.; the percentage of flour from other cereals to be mixed with wheaten flour shall be as fixed by the Flour Mills Control Committee from time to time.

Barley, maize, oats, rye, rice and beans are the permitted cereals from which flour may be manufactured as admixtures to wheaten flour. Soya bean flour is also permitted, but is limited to 5%.

The maximum retail price of maize flour, maize flakes, maize semolina, hominy, cerealine or maize meal is 3½d. per lb.; and of oatmeal, rolled oats, flaked oats or other like products of oats, 4½d. per lb. in Scotland, and 5d. per lb. elsewhere in the United Kingdom.

No person shall, without a permit issued under the authority of the Food Controller, sell any wheat, barley, oats or rye of the 1917 crop grown in the United Kingdom. All existing contracts are cancelled, except in such cases as the Food Controller shall otherwise determine, or in the case of contracts made by any Government Department.

The Food Controller has taken over all flour mills of the United Kingdom which use wheat in the making of flour, except those with an output of less than five sacks of flour per hour. These smaller mills will be taken over as from August 11th.

[*Manufacture of Flour and Bread Order (No. 2)* 1917, No. 187; *Manufacture of Flour and Bread Order (No. 3)* 1917, No. 315; *Flour Mills Order*, 1917, No. 377; *Bread Order*, 1917, No. 189; *Bread Order*, 1917, No. 483; *Wheat, Barley and Oats (Prices Order)*, 1917, No. 363; *Wheat, Rye and Rice (Restriction) Order*, 1917, No. 376; *Maize, Barley and Oats (Restriction) Order*, 1917, No. 404; *Oats and Maize Products (Retail Prices) Order*, 1917, No. 429; *Ditto, No. 2, No. 482; The 1917 Crop (Restriction) Order*, 1917, No. 721.]

CAKES AND PASTRIES.

The making of any light fancy pastries, muffins, crumpets, and other light articles of food is prohibited.

Cakes, buns, scones and biscuits, must conform to certain requirements as to the amount of sugar and wheaten flour that may be used.

15% of sugar is allowed in cakes and biscuits; 10% in buns. No sugar may be used in scones.

Not more than 30% of wheaten flour may be used in cakes, and 50% in buns and scones.

No ornamented cake or bun may be made.

[*Cake and Pastry Order*, 1917, No. 372.]

CHEESE.

The Food Controller has taken over all Cheese imported from the United States, Canada, Australia and New Zealand.

The Board of Trade has placed a quantity of Cheese on the market at a price which enables retailers to sell at 1/4 per lb.

[*Cheese (Requisition) Order*, 1917, No. 510.]

Controller may authorise if, after the crop has been gathered, it appears that the price is not such as will yield the growers a reasonable profit.

Growers whose total crop of Scottish raspberries does not exceed 1 cwt. are exempt.

[*Stone Fruit (Jam Manufacturers' Prices) Order*, 1917, No. 694; *Raspberries (Jam Manufacturers' Prices) Order*, 1917, No. 702; *Raspberries (Scotland) Delivery Order*, 1917, No. 703.]
S.66

HOARDING.

No person shall acquire supplies of food beyond the needs of his ordinary consumption.

A tradesman shall not sell any article of food where he has reasonable grounds for believing that the quantity ordered is in excess of requirements.

The Food Controller may order the inspection of premises in which he has reason to believe that hoarding is taking place.

[*Food Hoarding Order*, 1917, No. 317.]

HORSE RATIONING.

Restrictions are imposed on the feeding of horses with cereal foodstuffs. Hay, straw, bran, or dried brewers' grains are still allowable.

These restrictions do not apply to horses used exclusively for purposes of the Army Council or Admiralty, or in agriculture, stallions used for stud purposes, thoroughbred brood mares, and brood mares in foal or with foal at foot.

In the case of horses used for trade or business purposes, and of certain classes of thoroughbreds, a ration is fixed, the amount of which may be ascertained from the Order.

All other horses are precluded from receiving any cereal foodstuffs, except those mentioned in the first paragraph.

[*Horses (Rationing) Order*, 1917, No. 439.]

CONDITION OF SALE.

No trader, in selling an article, may impose a condition relating to the purchase of any other article.

[*Food (Conditions of Sale) Order*, 1917, No. 261.]

FRUIT.

No jam manufacturer shall buy, for preserving or bottling, any of the following fruits grown in the United Kingdom at prices exceeding those specified: Egg Plums, £10 10s. 0d. per ton; other plums, £12 10s. 0d. per ton; Farleigh or Kent Damsons, £12 0s. 0d. per ton; Pin, or Prune, or other Damsons, £14 0s. 0d. per ton; Greengages, £22 0s. 0d. per ton. No Raspberries shall be bought by a jam manufacturer for preserving or for the making of essence at a price exceeding £35 per ton.

These prices include picking and packing, and are f.o.r. or f.o.b., but where the fruit is delivered by the seller to the purchaser's premises, or for sale in a market, the customary charges may be added. Other permitted charges are the market tolls actually paid, and not more than 25s. a ton for the use of tubs, baskets or usual packages other than sacks. The commission of an Agent buying on behalf of a manufacturer is limited to 12s. 6d. per ton for the stone fruit and 20s. per ton for raspberries.

It is an offence to offer such fruit to a jam manufacturer at prices in excess of the above, or to enter into any fictitious transaction.

All raspberries grown in Scotland shall, as picked, be delivered to the Food Controller by the grower in accordance with the instructions of Mr. J. M. Hodge, Blairgowrie, nominated by the Food Controller for the purpose. Those in good condition will be paid for at the maximum price mentioned above, subject to any revision of price which the Food

MEAT SALES.

A person, called the dealer, who buys any fat cattle may only resell them to a person, called the permitted buyer, who undertakes to slaughter them within 14 days. This undertaking must be entered in a book kept at the market where the sale takes place, or, in other cases, on an authorised form, which must be sent by the dealer to the nearest market authority. Market Authorities may grant licences under certain conditions for a second dealer, called the distributing dealer, to purchase fat cattle for removal to another specified market for sale to a permitted buyer.

In respect to dead meat it is provided that a salesman, that is a person who has bought any dead meat, may sell it only to a retailer or a consumer and his profit is limited by the order.

All persons engaged in the production, purchase, sale, distribution, transport, storage or shipment of any cattle or meat, shall furnish such particulars as to their businesses as may from time to time be specified by or on behalf of the Food Controller, and shall verify the same in such manner as he may direct.

Rams, ewes, wethers, lambs, deer, goats and swine are included in the expression "Cattle" in addition to cattle usually so called.

[*Meat (Sales) Order*, 1917, No. 520; *Cattle and Meat (Returns) Order*, 1917, No. 767.]

MILK.

The maximum wholesale price of milk is 6½d. per imperial gallon and the retail price 2d. a quart over the price on the 15th of the same month in 1914.

[*Price of Milk Order*, 1917, No. 68; *Price of Milk Order (No. 2)*, 1917, No. 160.]

POTATOES.

No person shall, without a permit issued under the authority of the Food Controller, sell any potatoes of the 1917 crop, grown in the United Kingdom, other than first and second earlies. All existing contracts are cancelled, except in such cases as the Food Controller shall otherwise determine, or in the case of contracts made by any Government Department.

[*The 1917 Crop (Restriction) Order*, 1917, No. 721.]

PUBLIC MEALS.

Hotels, restaurants, clubs, boarding houses where the number of bedrooms for letting exceeds ten, and refreshment places generally are rationed in bulk according to the ascertained weekly average of meals served in them. The allowance of meat is based on an average of 5 ozs. for each luncheon and dinner, and 2 ozs. for each breakfast served; bread, 2 ozs. for each breakfast, luncheon, tea, and dinner, with 1 oz. of flour for each luncheon and dinner; and sugar, 2/7ths of an ounce for each breakfast, luncheon, tea, and dinner.

Establishments at which no meal is served costing more than 1s. 3d. exclusive of beverages, are not rationed. But where a public eating place is excluded from the Public Meals Order by reason of the fact that it never charges more than 1s 3d. for any meal, it shall not serve any individual between the hours of 3 p.m. and 6 p.m. with more than 2 ozs. in all of bread and cakes. This does not apply to places which limit to 6d. the maximum price charged for any meal served between the hours of 3 p.m. and 6 p.m. and not containing meat, fish or eggs.

[*Public Meals Order*, 1917, No. 445; *Ditto, No. 3, No. 664; Cake and Pastry Order*, 1917, No. 372.]

SUGAR.

No chocolate must be sold or bought retail at a price exceeding 3d. per oz., or any other sweetmeats at a price exceeding 2d. per oz.

The quantity of sugar used by manufacturers other than of jam, marmalade or condensed milk, is reduced to 25% of the 1915 supply.

[*Sugar (Confectionery) Order*, 1917, No. 65; *Sugar (Restriction) Order*, 1917, No. 281; *Ditto, No. 3, No. 458.*]

TEA AND COFFEE.

No tea may be packed other than the net weight.

All tea sold retail, whether contained in a package or not, shall be sold by net weight.

By arrangement with the trade, 25% of the total imports of tea from India and Ceylon is allocated to be sold to the public retail at 2s. 4d. per lb., 35% at 2/8, and 30% at 3s. The balance of 10% may be sold free from control.

An arrangement has also been made with the Coffee Trade Association to supply a good, sound, pure Coffee at a rate which would enable grocers to sell retail at 1s. 6d. per lb.

[*Tea (Net Weight) Order*, 1917, No. 318.]

ENFORCEMENT OF ORDERS.

Any infringement of an Order made by the Food Controller is a summary offence under the Defence of the Realm Regulations, and the offender is liable to imprisonment for six months, with or without hard labour, or a fine of £100, or both.

Contraventions of the Orders can in all cases be investigated and prosecuted by the police, and, in the case of those provisions with which the public are most directly concerned, by the local authorities.

BAKEWELL RURAL DISTRICT.

THE MEAT (MAXIMUM PRICES) ORDER, 1917.

The LOCAL FOOD COMMITTEE for the area of the Bakewell Rural District HEREBY GIVE NOTICE that they have this day (10th November, 1917), pursuant to the powers conferred on them by the above Order, prescribed that on and from THURSDAY, the 15th day of November, and until further notice, the following scale of MAXIMUM PRICES shall be applicable to sales of MEAT by retail in, about, or from any premises situated within their area, namely:—

SCALE OF MAXIMUM RETAIL PRICES.

	s.	d.	
BEEF:			
Ribs and Sirloin	1	4½	per lb.
Rounds and Rumps	1	4½	,,
Thick Flank	1	3½	,,
Thick Flat Ribs	1	3½	,,
Thin Flank	1	0½	,,
Boneless Beef	1	0½	,,
Bosom and Shin	1	2½	,,
Brisket Lap	1	1	,,
Brisket	0	10	,,
Neck End	0	9½	,,
Rump Steak	1	7½	,,
Second Steak	1	3½	,,
Kidney	0	10½	,,
Suet	0	8½	,,
MUTTON:			
Legs and Loin	1	5	,,
Shoulders and Best Neck..	1	3	,,
Breasts and Neck End ...	0	11	,,
Chops	1	6	,,
Suet	0	8	,,
PORK:			
Loins	1	6½	,,
Legs	1	5½	,,
Fillet	1	6½	,,
Shoulders	1	4½	,,
Hock	0	8½	,,
Chap	0	10½	,,

NOTICE IS HEREBY FURTHER GIVEN that no Meat may be sold by retail, in, about, or from any premises situate within the area of the Committee, at prices in excess of the above schedules, but lower prices may be charged. The Committee desire to call the attention of Butchers and other persons dealing in the sale of Meat by retail to certain provisions of the Meat Order, particulars of which may be obtained at the Local Food Office, as to Price Lists being posted in shops, as to records of dealings in Meat, and as to limitation of aggregate prices.

Infringements are summary offences against the Defence of the Realm Regulations.

By Order.

GEO. ALLSOP,
Executive Officer.

BAKEWELL RURAL DISTRICT LOCAL FOOD CONTROL COMMITTEE.

MILK PRICES ORDER 1917.

NOTICE IS HEREBY GIVEN that the LOCAL FOOD COMMITTEE have amended the MAXIMUM PRICE applicable to the Sale of Milk by Retail within the area of the above Rural District to:—

5½d. PER QUART,

to include all charges for delivery.

Such prices to remain in force from the 10th day of JANUARY, 1918, until otherwise determined by the Committee.

By Order,

GEO. ALLSOP,
Executive Officer.

Local Food Office,
Buxton-road, Bakewell

Telegraphic Address: "Foodagri., Vic., London."
Telephone: Victoria 3023.

Joint Committee Leaflet, No. 10.   **L.G. (Grain) 1.**

Issued on behalf of the Ministry of Food by the Joint Committee—Board of Agriculture and Ministry of Food.

THE CEREALS (RESTRICTION) ORDER, 1918.

IMPORTANT TO
Farmers, Stock-Keepers, Pig-Owners, Poultry-Keepers & Others.

1. The Food Controller has made an Order dated August, 1918, as to the sale and use of :—
WHEAT.   RYE.   BARLEY.   DREDGE CORN.
(Including TAILINGS, DRESSINGS AND SCREENINGS.)

2. This Order has been made because it is urgently necessary to save for human consumption all grain of this kind that is fit for the purpose and so to release ships for the transport of men and munitions.

3. The Order is printed in full at the back of this Notice and should be read carefully.
This leaflet is meant to explain to growers of grain and to persons wishing to feed grain to animals, how the Order chiefly affects them.

GRAIN FIT FOR HUMAN CONSUMPTION.

4. Grain of the kinds described above, if fit for human consumption, may not be fed to animals, and may be sold only to :—
  (i) A miller buying for the purpose of a Controlled Flour Mill.
  (ii) A recognised Dealer in grain.
  (iii) A person requiring or holding a licence for the purpose of manufacture.
  (iv) In the case of grain suitable for seed, a person buying such grain for the purpose of seed.
In selling grain for seed under this Order farmers and others must comply with the Testing of Seeds Order, 1918, and any other Order affecting the sale of seeds.

GRAIN UNFIT FOR HUMAN CONSUMPTION.

5. The Order forbids the feeding of grain of the kinds described above to any animal, unless a licence has been obtained. Exception is made in the case of persons buying unfit grain for this purpose in lots of 10 cwts. or less. In such cases the person selling the grain is responsible for getting a certificate of its unfitness before he sells it.

HOW TO GET A CERTIFICATE OR LICENCE FOR UNFIT GRAIN.

6. A farmer or other person wanting to *sell* grain that is unfit for human consumption in quantities of 10 cwts. or less should obtain a form of application (Form G. 1.) for a certificate from :—
  (i) The Local Food Office ; or
  (ii) The Grain Officer at the Corn Exchange, or Grain Market, on recognised Market days ; or
  (iii) The Divisional Food Commissioner, or a Grain Officer authorised by him.
These forms can be obtained (and returned) personally or through the post.

7. Persons proposing to sell grain that is unfit for human consumption in quantities exceeding 10 cwts. need not obtain a certificate.

8. Farmers or other persons wanting to *feed* grain that is unfit for human consumption to animals (except when they have bought such grain in a lot of 10 cwts. or less) must obtain in the same way a form of application (Form G. 2.) for a licence.

9. Every application must be accompanied by a sample of the grain in question. Each sample must be in an ordinary unglazed sample bag with the name and address of the applicant, the quantity and description of the bulk to which the sample relates, and the date of the application clearly written either on the bag itself, on a label securely attached to it. The Ministry of Food is obtaining a supply of bags for this purpose, and these will be issued to Grain Officers as soon as they are delivered by the manufacturers. As a further safeguard a slip of paper containing applicant's name and details of the grain should, if possible, be enclosed inside the bag with the grain.

10. The Food Controller trusts that farmers will recognise that this Order is made in view of a grave national need, and that they will assist him by loyally observing its provisions. In securing its observance he desires to cause as little inconvenience to farmers as possible. He is making, through the Divisional Food Commissioners, arrangements for the prompt grant of certificates and licences. If in any district farmers experience difficulty in getting their applications dealt with, they are asked to write and tell their Food Commissioner.

NOTE.—Copies of this leaflet may be obtained free of charge and post free on application to :—*The Secretary, Joint Committee of the Board of Agriculture and Ministry of Food, 6a, Dean's Yard, Westminster, S.W. 1,* and envelopes so addressed need not be stamped.

August, 1918.   MINISTRY OF FOOD.

M1042 Wt 22351/F41SA 680,000 8/18 MCC. N. (378)   **[P.T.O.**

R.G. 7.

MINISTRY OF FOOD.

MEAT RATIONING ORDER, 1918, AND OTHER RATIONING ORDERS, 1917-1918.—SELF-SUPPLIERS AND DIRECT SUPPLIES.

This memorandum is intended for general circulation, and is issued in place of the memoranda on Self-Suppliers (M.G.R.M. 9 and R.M. 17), referred to in the list of documents (M.G.R.M. 3) sent to Food Control Committees.

1

This Memorandum deals with the application of the rationing system to Self-Suppliers, that is to say persons producing meat or butter for home consumption and with the control of Direct Supplies, that is to say supplies sent direct from the producer to the consumer and not through a registered retailer.

2

The consumption of rationed food by Self-Suppliers will be regulated in three distinct ways, according to the animal or food concerned, namely :—

I. Rabbits and Hares,

II. Cattle, Sheep and Pigs,

III. Poultry, Game Birds and Wild Fowl, Venison, and Butter.

3

Consumption in Class I. (Rabbits and Hares) by Self-Suppliers will be uncontrolled (pars. 15-16).

4

Consumption in Class II. (Cattle, Sheep and Pigs) will be controlled by Reports of Slaughter. The general principle will be (1) to require the owner of the animal to report the slaughter to the Food Office within seven days with necessary particulars, and (2) to require the head of the household consuming the meat to account for the consumption by coupons at the rate appropriate in each case (pars. 17-21).

5

Consumption in Class III. (Poultry, Game Birds and Wild Fowl, Venison, and Butter) will after July 13th be controlled by registration of "Self-Supplying Households." Till then, the head of the household will be responsible for keeping records of food so consumed and for marking butter cards or detaching, cancelling and keeping coupons from meat cards and supplementary cards, so as to account for the rationed foods consumed at the rate appropriate in each case (pars. 22-28).

6

The appropriate rate for accounting for consumption in each case is set out in the Table of Coupon Rates for Self-Suppliers at the end of this Memorandum. Briefly the position is as follows : The meat of pigs, game birds and wild fowl, and butter may be consumed by self-suppliers at special rates in excess of the ordinary ration, and the meat of rabbits and hares may be consumed in addition to the ration. No special advantage is given to self-suppliers in respect of cattle, sheep, venison and poultry, that is to say the appropriate rate is approximately the same as that applicable to the general population under the ration scale.

7

The right of consumption on self-suppliers' terms applies not only to the actual producer in each case (as defined in par. 9), but also to his household and certain classes of employees (par. 10). It does not, except to the extent mentioned in paragraph 12, apply to establishments of any kind (residential establishments, catering establishments, institutions), even though the food is obtained direct from a farm controlled by the head of the establishment. Such food must be accounted for at the ordinary rate as Direct Supplies.

2061 Wt. _ /G1159. 6, 6, 12 pfs. 3,000. 2,000,000. 4/18. S.O.,F.Rd

8

The obtaining of Direct Supplies will after July 13th be controlled by Direct Supply Permits. Till then the head of the household obtaining such supplies will be responsible for seeing that a corresponding reduction is made in purchases of rationed food from other sources and for marking butter cards or detaching, cancelling, and keeping coupons from meat cards or supplementary cards so as to account for the supplies obtained at the ordinary rate (pars. 29-34).

PERSONS QUALIFIED TO CONSUME AS SELF-SUPPLIERS.

9

The following persons are entitled to rank as producers, and to consume their produce on self-supplier's terms accordingly :—

(a) In respect of the meat or produce of a tame animal, the person owning the animal, provided that he has owned it for not less than two months before slaughter in the case of cattle, sheep, and pigs, or one month in any other case, and that he is either the occupier of, or resides on, or has in the ordinary course of his trade acquired grazing rights over, the land or other premises where the animal is kept.

(b) In respect of the meat of a wild animal, the person lawfully killing or capturing it, either in person or by his employees or guests or members of his household.

10

The following persons, in addition to the actual producers in each case may consume on self-supplier's terms :—

(i.) All persons forming part of the same household as the producer, including domestic servants and temporary guests ;

(ii.) Persons habitually fed in the same household as the producer, though not residing there ;

(iii.) Persons and the dependents of persons employed by the producer on agricultural work or on the capture or maintenance of animals used for food, who, though not forming part of his household or habitually taking meals there, receive meat or butter from him as a matter of custom.

Consumption by the producer or any of these persons is described below as consumption in the household of the producer or in the self-supplying household.

11

The producer need not necessarily reside on the farm or other premises where the animal is kept, killed or captured. The self-supplier's privilege covers both him and others residing with him and forming part of his household at any place.

12

The extension of the self-supplier's privilege in the foregoing paragraphs does not apply to establishments (whether residential establishments, catering establishments, or institutions). Where, for instance, a farm is owned or worked by or on behalf of an asylum, workhouse, hospital, school, hotel etc., the persons living in such establishments cannot consume the produce except

Wormhill Tales - Claude

In wartime days, Little Alfy was the postman; he had a push bike with a front carrier frame for the post bag and parcels. As Christmas approached his load got bigger and bigger. Some farmers from outlying farms, while bringing their children to school, would wait for Alf and take any post back with them which helped a great deal.

Alfy on the right.

Now at Christmas the village postman was given a drink at most calls, mainly sherry but sometimes something stronger at some of the bigger farms. So by the time that Alfy got to Mrs Wains, the last call, he would be plastered.

Mrs Wain's cooking and baking was exceptional and at Christmas 1944 she gave him a glass of homemade wine and some mince pies. Alfy managed the wine alright but he was having a tough time with his mince pie. *'By gum missus, your mince pies are tough.'* He said, biting at the offending pie without much success. In those days it was common to make them in individual tins and poor Alfy was trying to eat it with the tin still on!

By this time it would be late afternoon and normally, with Wains being the last of four farms at Wormhill Meadow, the postman would make his way back to Millers Dale via Flag Dale, lifting the bike over the stiles; it was rough going but much shorter. But at this time of the year it was going dark and with the intoxicated state of Alfy they thought it would be better to load him into a van with bike and bags and return him to Millers Dale station where they loaded him and his baggage on to the train back to Buxton. The railway men at the other end were warned by telegraph that Alfy was on the train and would need helping off and pointing in the direction of the General Post Office!

Mrs K at Hill Green had a chimney that didn't draw very well and the angles of the flue made it difficult to use a brush. So she would get her son-in-law to take a bag to work and fill it with gunpowder; he worked in the quarry. With the wind in the right direction and the fire out, she got a cast iron oven shelf, laid it on the fire hole, nice and level, poured out a heap of gunpowder on this plate with a trickle away from it like a slow fuse across the kitchen floor to the door and then lit it. After a minute it would go off-woof, and the chimney was cleared.

You couldn't get gunpowder during the war but after the war, he decided to get mother-in-law some more powder. The bag may have been heavier than before but he didn't notice. Mrs K did the same as before, put a match to the powder but it wouldn't light, so she put a second match in the powder while the brimstone was still fizzing. It worked but instead of going woof it went BANG. You'd expect a black face, but she was alright, but when she went round the back of the house, the fireplace had stopped where it was and the back wall had been blown out; this new powder was much more powerful.

Bonfire night comes once a year, a good job too. In the not too distant past, it was a night of reckoning - old scores were settled. As the village bonfire burnt lower, young men, and sometimes women too, went round the village quietly lifting gates off, sometimes exchanging

On the Flatt, 1963.
Peter, Elizabeth and Stephen Taylor.

LEFT: At the Bagshawe Arms. Les Wilshaw centre.

Wormhill Mothers' Union Party 1950s.

them for someone else's, so there was a lot of sorting out to do the next morning. If there was a special score to settle the gates were thrown into the village pond followed by carts and traps, anything they could get their hands on-even the Constable's bike got thrown in one night after he'd been a bad spoilsport.

With it being a quarry area, there was gunpowder to be had for the making of fireworks. One farmer had a special way to make what he called a cannon. For this he used a 56lb weight, the kind coal wagons used to carry round to check the weight of coal. He packed the hollow in the weight with black powder and put a fuse in it to suit the occasion. He was a Special Constable as well and would be back in uniform when the old ladies in the area played up when the 'cannon' had gone off - and reported it to him.

One particular bonfire night the constable for the area had come on his bike from Peak Dale to keep an eye on us at Wormhill. He was stood in a corner where he could watch everyone. However earlier in the day the cannon maker had put his cannon in the bottom of the drystone wall on the other side from where the constable was standing. At the right moment, he lit the long fuse, escaped home, changed quickly back into uniform and just got back in time to see the explosion and the constable going end over end up the road. He was lucky not to be hurt; his uniform was torn.

Some of us were annoyed at a trick like that, so we carted him off to the Bagshawe Arms to soothe his nerves. He could have caused a lot of trouble but he didn't. He often came into the tap room at the end of his round at closing time. He looked at everyone and if there was someone he didn't like, he cleared them off, then he'd say, *'Drink up, it's time you were out of here,'* ordering a pint for himself at the same time. Many times if there were only a few in, he would pay for the round, he didn't like drinking on his own. After maybe 12 pints and at 2am perhaps, there were times I put his bike in the back of my home-made truck and carted him back to Peak Dale. But if I saw the Superintendent about, I carried straight on through and parked somewhere in Batham Gate and waited till I saw his car go past for Buxton, then dropped the constable back at home. He was well liked.

Millers Dale station as I remember it was a big, busy and important place. All the express 'through' trains stopped there. The station yard is now cleared of its cattle loading ramps and pens. Gone are the sidings for goods wagons to unload coal for the area; corn for Dakins Mills, one near to the Railway Hotel and the other near the

Anglers Rest. Other feed supplies for the farms like stock feed potatoes and other root crops. And silk used to come for the winding mill at Litton. And in bad weather, people sent their churns of milk by train as they had done prior to the milk lorries.

There was a weighbridge where goods were weighed in or out such as steel for the quarries or building materials. There were cab stands for cars picking up passengers. Between the station yard and platforms were wrought iron railings and an iron gate to the station proper with its ticket office, waiting rooms and parcel office.

There were 5 platforms; No 1 was Manchester to London, 2, London to Manchester, 3 and

Constructing the second viaduct at Millers Dale.

Construction workers and steam engine with Millers Dale Quarry in background.

Constructing the second viaduct at Millers Dale.

Millers Dale station.

4, local trains and 5 Buxton only. The Buxton trains to Millers Dale stopped at Blackwell Mill by request, said to be the smallest station in Britain.

Across No 1 platform onto the track, now stripped of its rails, sleepers, chairs, points and signal furniture, are the viaducts which had an armed guard on them all through the war. We believe there were several attempts to attack them including one night when two land mines were dropped - the turbulence around the peaks may have caused the parachutes on them to float off course and drop at Priestcliffe 1000 yards away. So the road and railway, like the river Wye, kept on flowing, carrying thousands of tons of war hardware and troop trains by the score.

After the viaducts is the now closed quarry, a battery of lime kilns and the bed where a boiler used to stand which created power to run the compressors used in the quarry. About 1914, the boiler exploded. It was said the explosion was heard miles away and that if the London express had been passing at the time it could have blown it off the track - it would have rolled right down into the river. Ever after that all boilers had to have a ministry safety test every year. Next was the crusher and then open countryside.

Above the valley, before the war, two special pylons were erected to carry high voltage electric wires which spanned the dale and at the time were the longest in Britain. In the valley, the scars are healing, the sides clothed in ash trees, hazel groves and other vegetation down to the glistening white cliffs of Ravenstor. After a few hundred yards, you can see Tideswell Dale. In my schooldays, the school bus used to go from Litton Mill up that dale.

Quarries are not just a mess on the landscape; there are many meaningful parts. The office staff and the light duty gang, who man the weighing bridges, move stock from the main stores, look after the horses and more. Then the tough quarry men - the fillers, getters, poppers, plate layers, those responsible for removing the overburden, and the ones running the kilns.

One very cold frosty morning the cleaner called out to Mr. Hallam that she would have some pancakes ready soon, thinking he would stop on his way back. But no, he stopped immediately and, going into the warm cabin to wait, after a couple of minutes he had a warm pancake on his plate. He loved pancakes and by the time he had eaten the first one another was ready. As he was eating the second a charge-hand called him out to get the waggons moving. *'Yer'll 'ave wait till av finished me ponkit,'* he replied. Eventually, in his own time, he went out to where his horses were. Getting hold of the bridle of the lead horse, he said *'Come on'* but she did not move - the waggons were frozen to the rails. And that was how he got the nickname Pancake.

Many years later Tommy Teeboon was working for us at the Bagshawe Arms farm when an old gentleman went past, on his way to the post office to get his pension. When Tommy shouted 'Pancake!' the old gentleman stopped, looked all round and then waved his stick in the air, saying *'If you get this stick up your backside you will sprout!'*

Brindley Fountain and old post office at Wormhill.

Mr Redfern at Miller's Dale Quarry (East Buxton).   Thought to be quarrymen from Chelmorton.

'Staffordshire Farmers' workmen 1950s.
George Mycock, Ernest Hollingdrake, Cliff Hancock, Peter Cartledge, Dennis Pedley.

Railway men at
Millers Dale.

Wormhill 1938.
J. Wilshaw,
Alec Elliot,
Bill Holland,
John Samuel Wilde.

Signal box at
Millers Dale.

Glebe Farm seen from Millers Dale viaduct.

Drawing eyes at Millers Dale quarry.

ABOVE: Mary Mellor and Robin Taylor.

LEFT: At Blackwell Hall

BELOW:
At Wormhill Well Dressing, horse judging, 1950.
Foreground L to R: Lol Gibson, Robert Taylor,
Walter Warhurst, Fred Percival.

Above: Noel Taylor on the
Flatt, Wormhill 1950s.

Right:
Les Wilshaw at Middle Hills
near Wormhill.

Below:
Wormhill Moor late 1940s.
Noel Taylor and son Robert.

Dance at Wormhill Village Hall 1950.

Wormhill Well Dressing Queen 1951 or 52.
Pam Beresford, Mavis Beresford, Margaret Teebon, Marion Mellor, Sylvia Skidmore, Elizabeth Taylor.

John Mycock

I was born in 1933 at Bubnell, then we moved back to where dad was born, Manor Farm, Blackwell on March 25th 1939. Lots of Chatsworth tenants changed farms that day, which rarely occurred from that time onwards; very few people moved on the estate after '39. On the same day, Percy Longden came to Blackwell from Martinside. There were four main families in Blackwell at that time.

My mother suffered from depression off and on through her life; she had fallen in Cheedale when she was 16 and knocked her head and had problems ever after. She lost twins in 1940 and had to go into hospital in Sheffield during the Blitz which didn't help. So I went to Chelmorton to live with my granny and went to school there. I was left-handed and one of the teachers, Miss Mckevvit would insist that I wrote with my right hand and she would hit me over the knuckles with a ruler. This caused me to start copying from my desk mate, Graham Wheeldon and I developed a stutter. Luckily, I was only there for 6 months and then went to Taddington School where there was a teacher, Miss Simpson who recognised that I'd got problems and encouraged my good subjects, taking little notice of my poor subjects like reading and writing - I was bottom of the class at spelling. This boosted my confidence.

As a little boy, I'd had bantams and discovered an interest in poultry which led to father saying he wouldn't pay me a wage for work on the farm but I could keep as many poultry as I wished. In wartime we only had oats, we didn't grow anything else, which poultry are not very fond of. So I fed potatoes and things like that to help keep them warm in wintertime and encourage them to lay, because eggs were scarce in winter; you had to put them away in isinglass or lime when there were plenty, for winter use.

I was trying to do this in the '47 snow and succeeded by providing them with heat and light from a Tilley lamp. I was quite proud of getting them to lay through the Big Snow. I'd half fill the Tilley so that it would give them 3 hours, then burn itself out. If I fed them when I took the lamp in, they would get off the perches and eat and then be back on by the time the lamp went out. I gave them some purchased wheat with added condiment and limestone dust to help keep the eggshells strong. The condiment was called Carrswood Poultry Spice and was a red-brown spicy smelling powder which came in a 7lb tin with a little ladle. It was a secret formula and there was a competitor called Ovum. Once I'd tried it, I swore by it, the poultry liked it and seemed to thrive.

I did well enough out of the eggs to buy a new van after 5 years. Ormes, from Bakewell used to have the eggs to sell; a man used to pick them up. He had an Austin 7 and he could get 7 cases of eggs in it. He also got work on the farms as an electrician. Electricity came early to Blackwell before the war whereas over the river at Wormhill it was the early 1950s.

We were bombed twice during the war; once with incendiaries the night Earl Sterndale church was bombed and some were dropped at Wormhill. It's thought they were trying for Millers Dale Viaduct. One dropped between our house and next door and I remember father throwing the contents of the cinders bucket on it. Another time two big bombs were dropped at Priestcliffe. They were one ton land mines dropped on huge parachutes. The roof blew off one farmhouse while the farmer lay in bed; luckily no-one was really hurt. There was a searchlight division on Taddington moor and they were after the plane.

During the '47 snow, we had a man working for us who smoked a lot. One night he said, *'I'll milk the cows for you if you'll fetch me some fags from the Waterloo.'* It was blizzarding

At Bubnell 1936. John Mycock as a little boy.

RIGHT: Dad and Harry Handley at Bubnell.

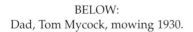

BELOW:
Dad, Tom Mycock, mowing 1930.

as it did many nights and what you'd dug out during the day was blown back in again. There were still some German prisoners of war based at Bakewell and they dug out the A6 every day for a couple of months. It was about 8 foot deep, so you walked through a narrow gap enough to get a lorry through. They had to keep it open to get coal to Lancashire from the Derbyshire coal field on army lorries. The railways were closed and it was easier to keep the roads open using the German prisoners; they succeeded mostly, getting a convoy of lorries through before it blew in again.

So I was trying to get up to the Waterloo at 7 o'clock at night; I'd no torch and the snow was so fine you breathed it in. It was so cold that it blew like sand. I knew I'd got 200 yards between the Dukes Plantations on the main road and if I kept going I'd get through. I got my breath in the shelter of the plantations. If I had stopped, I should never have got going again. I suppose it was a daft thing to do, just for some cigarettes.

We had to fetch bread from Taddington, if it got through, but we went without coal and stuff, though we'd eggs and bacon enough for every meal. I used to go to bed at night and throw all the clothes from the wardrobe over the bed because we lived in a draughty farmhouse. The jerry under the bed would be frozen in the morning; quite common.

During the 1800s the Duke of Devonshire owned a lot of Buxton and was in the habit of taking the waters regularly. So he planted the trees in the regular plantations beside the A6 between Taddington and Topley to make the journey to Buxton more scenic. On an old map of 1820 which I have a copy of, it shows the trees in the area of Blackwell and there were very few. It seems very open and possibly moorland; some of the fields are called moors whereas now it's green and idyllic. In 1812 they dug out the road down Topley Pike; before that they had to go down to Blackwell Mill and go by the riverside. I remember a man called Millward who was employed by the Duke as a waller, and his father planted the plantations and built the walls around them.

When we were lads, I helped them take the sheep from Blackwell Hall down to the sheepwash in Cheedale. I stayed all afternoon helping. There was Bill Gregory, his brother and me helping the three men to wash the sheep. We were helping to pen them; it wasn't a proper enclosure then, just some netting on top of a fallen down wall. They were Oxfords, big docile sheep and if any escaped we had to keep them gathered. There was a small pen next to the river for the men to catch them in and put them in the river. There had to be a man standing in the river to wash the sheep and then guide them back up the bank. It was usually done on a Saturday when there were lads like us to help.

I could run to my granny at Chelmorton in 20 minutes-up Pillwill and over the fields and also to my other granny at Wormhill in 20 minutes down the fields and over the river in Cheedale. At one stage over half the population of Wormhill were related to me. It's one village that hasn't changed much over the years. My uncles, the Bagshawes who were at Brierlow Bar Garage, their family were joiners from Wormhill. They were related to me both through Mycocks and Taylors-twice over.

They started selling bikes and then motorbikes and sidecars in the 1920s before farmers around here could afford cars after horse and traps. Uncle Pym brought motorbikes into the yard - father wasn't keen. *'John, I've got you a motorbike; give me a deposit and pay me when you've got the money.'* He did that with two bikes and two vehicles- I was a lucky lad really. I had the 'poultry van' off him. In the 1930s they were selling cars and later tractors.

Sheepwashing in Cheedale.

Haymaking at Blackwell.

This was the earliest haymaking,
May 1961.

TOP:
On the 'new tractor' with
Grandad on the back, 1954
Manor Farm.

MIDDLE: Sheepwashing in
Cheedale, and on my
motorbike, 1951.

BOTTOM:
My new poultry van.

There were 7 sons and 5 worked at the garage; they were all characters and constantly falling out; if you didn't go to the right one for what you wanted, there'd be a row. Each one did a separate job - one on the pumps, one in the office, one doing tyres, one repairs, one selling cars. They all wanted to do the pumps so I think they had to have turns. Sunbeams were the main cars they liked to sell and they became agents for Kennings. And if you wanted to know anything, you'd go to Brierlow Bar garage - what wasn't known there wasn't worth knowing; everyone went for a chat. There was Fred, William (Pym), Sam (Hardy), Jack, Herbert (Foggy), Frank and Leonard. Pym got his nickname from Pimpo the clown because of his tricks like walking on stilts.

Old Hall Farm late 1930s. Winnie Turner, Annie Mycock (mum)
with John & Betty, Minnie & Esther Bagshawe, Sally Bagshawe.

Bagshawe Bros.

The White Peak Hunt at the Waterloo, Taddington, 1910.

The Bagshawe brothers garage
at Brierlow Bar.

DERBYSHIRE COUNTY COUNCIL
Road Traffic Acts, 1930 to 1936   No. 9979

PROVISIONAL DRIVING LICENCE

MR LEONARD JAMES BAGSHAWE,
of BRIERLOW BAR, BUXTON, DERBYS

is hereby licensed to drive MOTOR VEHICLES OF
ALL GROUPS

from 6 MAY 1945 until 15 MAY 1946 inclusive
subject to the condition prescribed in paragraph 4(1) & Regulation 16
of the Motor Vehicles (Driving Licences) Regulations, 1937 (SEE NOTE IN BOOK)

FEE OF   H. WILFRID SKINNER
5/-   Licence Officer
RECEIVED   New County Offices, Iron Gate, DERBY

USUAL SIGNATURE
OF LICENSEE ..... L J Bagshawe

Bagshawe Bros.
Brierlow Bar Garage.

Mary Lomas

There were 5 children in our family at Cowlow, I was the oldest, born in August 1925. When I was about 3, I went shopping with my mother - in those days you had to get the bus down on the A6, there was a rough cart road winding down to there and that was the way we walked to King Sterndale school. There was someone coughing and I started with this whooping cough and my little sister, Lily Ann, she got it and had to be nursed on a bed in the corner of this room. Dr Charlton visited her, eventually it turned to double pneumonia and she died aged 17 months.

After that I had trouble with my eyes and had to go to Manchester Eye Hospital for treatment and they gave me drops and sent me home, but after a while it would start again and I had to go again and they kept me in for 3 months. They used to turn my eyelids back and do this silver across the eye and they damaged my left eye and I've always had a stigma and not been able to see as well with that one.

Then there were William and Fred. At age 3, Fred had to go in Buxton Hospital for 6 months with a hip fracture. He was set in plaster in the children's ward. I can remember going with granny to look through this window at him because they said, *'You can't go in to see him, it would upset him too much.'* He had fair curly hair which we called 'cupid curls'.

The youngest was Elsie; she got peritonitis after a burst bowel. There was the trouble of getting the doctor, there was no telephone then, the workman had to fetch him. The doctor sent them to the Cottage Hospital, he got Mr Mycock from the Lower Farm to take them to Buxton; then they sent her on to Stockport where she had an operation, but she got Diptheria and died aged 5. I remember fetching the stirks in from round the back and sitting Elsie on the back of one - they were mard from being hand reared - and I pointed across the valley to King Sterndale telling her *'That's where you'll go to school.'* She said, *'I'm not going that place!'*

The Upper Farm was the Lomas homestead, dad was the eldest of 5 and Uncle Fred that farmed on Middle Farm was a younger one. Grandfather had bought the two farms in 1893. He was one of 7 sons and one daughter from Green Fairfield Farm. Dad said the two farms had cost something over £4,000. Dad and Uncle Fred had been farming the two farms as W & F Lomas but after a while with all these children, first one ailing and then another in hospital, the money was going in doctors' bills because they had to be paid then. So Fred said he'd farm the Middle Farm on his own. So they split the farms and made it 72 acres each. They used to say the Middle Farm was a pub at one time.

I remember the big quarry at Tunstead starting; they were running little jubilees across the top taking the waste to tip it down Blackwell Mill end. That was in 1930s and up to when the war was on, then they went onto mechanised modern machines.

It was 1946 when ICI came pestering; they managed to get the bottom farm which used to belong to John Duncombe's estate and then they came here; Uncle Fred sold to them and they came pestering dad. I can remember them coming into the house, the two directors, Mr Black and Mr Ryder. They sat with a bottle of whisky on the table negotiating how much they would pay. Uncle Fred had accepted £10,000. *'If you'll sell,'* they said, *'We'll give notice to quit to Mycocks on the Lower Farm and all that land we'll divide between these upper farms until the quarry takes it.'* So dad gave way and the whisky was served round and we've rented the farm from the quarry since. Dad wasn't happy; he had the two sons and wanted them to have the farm.

So Mycocks had a sale in 1947 and ICI came and divided the land up; I can remember them in the front room. Dad insisted on having the land on the bottom side so it wouldn't go to the quarry as fast; he had the Woo Dale land and Uncle Fred had the big dale that ran onto Blackwell Mill. So from 72 acres, we were farming 122, but both my brother and myself had left school.

The road up to the back pastures, what we call the 'Meres', they started pulling those plantations down. There was grazing up there, it was open to the quarry face and dad used to take the cows up to graze and sit with them before bringing them back to the fenced fields for safety and ready for morning.

Orient Lodge was up the road, Brittains had it built, I think in the 1890s. Their money was in tea plantations. There was the big house, cottages and a magnificent range of farm buildings which were used as a stud farm. Granddad used to build the walls round the plantations. Miss Brittain would leave her bike in one of our sheds while she went down to the A6 to get a bus. They used to have lads out of approved schools to work on the farm.

Mary

It's been terrible having the quarry taking the land away, taking our living, we've had to struggle so; the last bit of land they took, they only gave us £40 compensation which they knocked off the rent. When dad transferred the tenancy in 1963 to William, it should have come to me because I was the oldest but they said, *'We'd prefer to have a man rather than a woman.'* I've worked on the farm all my life, but I seem to have had a life of looking after my parents and then my brother Fred until he died.

I kept a lot of hens and sold the eggs, all free range. I paid for all the corn, hen cotes and everything out of it myself until the 1980s when the quarry came and planted more trees in the Big Meadow for screening and taking more land again. I thought there's no point me keep paying for the corn and there's nothing to live on, the eggs will have to go into the farm. So we kept more, then we had to have a grading machine. There was a good shop on Victoria Park at Fairfield, they had 100 dozen a week and the butcher sold some. I had about 500 hens and reared my own pullets from day old chicks.

Then in 1986 the shop at Fairfield sold the business and the new man said the eggs were too dear, even though they were sought after. So I had to go to Chelford Market with the eggs and that was a burden. Then that Edwina Curry put it out about eggs having salmonella and that finished the poultry job off along with the foxes coming out of the plantations in the daytime and fetching the hens. Luckily I was drawing my pension then and my brother was ill, so he had some social security and that kept us going.

The farms at Cowlow.

William Lomas

There was the quarry at Blacka Mill there, above the cottages - eight cottages in bottom and a bridle path up to Meadow Farm and one leading down into the quarry where the kilns were. Dad had a field beyond there, we called ICI field, 13 acres which ran down to Taylors Dale (Flagdale). We took the cattle up

Fred and William.

Bullend and down Tunstead to get to it. They kept the horses on it for the quarry and kept them at Wains at Meadow in winter. There was a siding under the kilns and the horses had to pull the big railway trucks from under the kilns and put them on the railway sidings ready for the trains to hook up to. Jim Stone at Tunstead Cottage worked them with three or four big shires.

Blackwell Mill Quarry (later Buxton Central).

David Garner

In 1955, I was apprenticed at Blacka Mill with the kiln brickies, I was 15. They were bad kilns there-no fans in 'em. They used let 'em out one day and expect brickies go in day after. Tunstead weren't so bad because there were big fans in to cool 'em and all heat went out top, but at Blacka Mill there were no fans.

There were four kilns; we had to re-line or repair 'em. ICI would say, *'Right, we're lettin' a kiln out at Blacka Mill, we want all t' men down there.'* And they'd draw it empty, all t' lime that were in, then inspect it, then we had to put all the scaffoldin' in; it were a big job. From bottom ter firing floor - them big arches where they spin the coal in with a machine. Then from there ter top of chimney, but very rare that bit would want repairin'. Tunstead kilns were bigger. When they were drawin' lime out at bottom, if they started drawin' bricks out they knew it was bad and you'd 'appen have do it all.

It had to be round scaffolding, same size as kiln, restin' on chain blocks so it could be lifted up and down. Jack Rogers was foreman and there were four shifts of men with always one shift restin'. As soon as they let 'em out, they had to be done as quick as possible and get 'em goin' agen. It was a bloody awful job there, we had a hosepipe in every firin' eye tryin' ter cool it. There were four firin' eyes and it was dryin' it up as it ran down the brickwork-there was no water runnin' off the bottom, it was all steam.

Firebricks used come in by rail inter a little sidin' and we used go down and load 'em inter jubilee trucks and you had a bell system - the rope-runner was in the haulage house, it was endless rope and you tightened a big screw up and it took it and a man stood at firin' floor level, pressed twice and it stopped while he unloaded.

The quarry there wasn't workin' then, all the stone came down from Tunstead on dumpers ter be tipped in a hopper and a bloke called Ev Nadin, it were his job with jubilees to draw the stone out of the bunker and tip it in the kilns. Coal came in trucks off the main line and they used empty it with elephants trunkin' about a foot in diameter and it sucked all the fine dusty coal up. I can see the man now - we used look out of firin' floor winder and he was on top o' these trucks and this trunkin' had big handles on and the power that had - it used suck the coal about 100 foot to the top; he'd empty a truck in less than an hour.

Cartoon by Roy Barber of Tideswell, of the union elections 1940s.
Top: Albert Garner (dad) who was later killed in the quarry.
Middle: Sam brewed tea in the cabin, the men paid him so much a week to brew - the 'rent'
Bottom: Ned Fletcher and Harry Hodgkinson.

When they used horses, every horse got a man's wage and when they were jiggered, they used fetch 'em back t' th' farm ter rest 'em and Jim Longden 'ud replace 'em. I can remember the chaps leadin' 'em up on a halter, three or four big ones and we used turn 'em out up Coopers Field. I were only a lad and Ron Salt 'ud say, *'Go and catch me such a horse.'* And we'd bring it down and he'd take 'em off down quarry.

I didn't stick the brickin' job long, about 2 years; it were limited, buildin' in a circle all t' time. I ended up lorry drivin'. I remember a feller called Jim Braddock, a filler at Hindlow and when I saw him in the quarry, he could fill 17 or 18 wagons in the day. A cabin lad used go round with yokes on his shoulders and two buckets o' gruel and he put the buckets down and Jim used say, *'Give us eowd o' t' bucket.'* And he'd sup nearly half a bucketful. Oatmeal, water and salt because they used sweat that much-they were wet through.

I've played in a band since I was nine, mostly Peak Dale Public Band and I'm still playing euphonium for them. As soon as we were able to play we went out on engagements; on Christmas Eve when everyone had finished work we set off round the Upper End part of Peak Dale with torches playing carols. You had to do the best you could to read the music; there were very few street lamps then and they were gas lamps. We finished at Great Rocks Club about 10 o'clock. Then on Christmas Day it was 8.30 start at the bottom end of the village, then the farms; Smalldale, the Fearns at Heath Farm, then Gorsey Nook, Higher Sydney and Lower Sydney which have all gone now, then down to Great Rocks finishing at the Midland Hotel. We finished about 4 o'clock, we missed our Christmas dinner to raise money for band funds and carried on even if it was raining or snowing. We enjoyed it, though it's said the women grumbled because the dinners were spoiling. For most people then, they only had Christmas Day and Boxing Day off work.

The coal vacuum.

The kilns at Blackwell
Mill Quarry
(Buxton Central).

Peak Dale Band, late 1940s.
Stan Garner, Jim Hulley Snr, Charlie Kitchen, Len Hoyle, Frank Needham, Lewis Middleton, Ken Turner, Bill Turner,
Ken Middleton, Reg Hallam, Phillip Hollister, Herbert Bradwell, Fred Eaton, Bill Mullins, Ted Morris, Jack Swann.
Front: Nigel Carter, David Garner, Geoff Owen, Arthur Beswick, Harry Beswick.

Peak Dale Band, late 1950s.

Arthur Nicholas Lomas

We lived at Chamber Farm, Peak Forest; it was 210 acres and the rent was £80 from the Duke. When I was about 12 we had a horse called Bony on the farm. They said he was an old war horse; I used to do chain harrowing with him. He was quite clever and got a reputation around the village. One day a woman turned up and a man with a camera from the Daily Express.

Mr Taylor, Wormhill.

She'd heard about this clever horse in the area that could communicate so I got him out and walked him round. She said, *'I've not seen any communication yet.'* I said, *'Ask him how old you are.'* She said, *'Bony, how old am I?'* so he lifted his tail and passed wind and stamped his foot twice. She said, *'What does that mean?'* *'Farty two!'*

Peak Forest.

Some fighting - Claude

As well as telling yarns and teaching me to sing some good and some naughty songs, granddad gave me some more education for life, his lessons in self defence. When we'd been sat in front of the fire for long enough, he'd get up saying, *'Get them gloves out and I'll go a round or two with you before dinner.'* As I got them out, I went rooting for my picture of Eddy Force in my toy box; my pin-up cut from the side of a corn flake box. Once I had Eddy in place where I could get inspiration from him, I was ready for battle. These bouts usually ended in tears, more of frustration and temper than hurt and getting over this was important. Both dad and granddad knew this and promoted this part of the training - the mind as well as the body.

When I was four or five, granddad put me on the kitchen table to bring me up to the same height as him. This was alright while he was in reach, so to even things up I'd get him to stand between the table and the wall. Now, I'd got him where I wanted or so I thought.

Wormhill with the Bagshawe Arms prominent centre left.

On 25th March 1939, we moved to the Bagshawe Arms Inn at Wormhill which had an 80 acre farm with it. The rent was £175 per annum. One reason for moving was because the school was nearby, a couple of hundred yards away in fact. So my three younger sisters never had to walk all the miles that I had done to and from school; I estimate 850 miles a year, and Sunday school and going to shops on top of that.

On the following Monday morning I was sent to Pursglove School, Tideswell, being 11 years old. During the morning break I was picked on with being the new boy and called names like *'another thick farmer'*. At lunchtime things got worse with several fights, but I must have been harder than they thought and things quietened down; then suddenly while I was stood in the toilet, one of them came up behind me and took a swing over my shoulder, hitting me on the mouth. I think he had something in his hand - I had cuts in my mouth from my teeth and a bad cut to my lip. I was taken to the first aid room to be cleaned up, where they checked my medical papers and found that I was a year too young to be at school. The headmaster apologised for his pupils and asked if I knew who had done it, which I didn't. He said no-one would admit to it and no-one else would tell, so that was the end of that.

So I went to Wormhill School for a while. Miss Davis was surprised to find that I couldn't write while being forward in history, geography, the Bible, mental arithmetic and reading. Both she and Mrs Savage taught me a lot in many ways; firstly never waste anything, be it time or materials; save and use every scrap of paper. No one at Wormhill had to have the back of their hands rapped with the sharp edge of a ruler leaving marks for the rest of their lives and mental scars that can't be seen.

Haymaking at Bagshawe Arms. Claude in middle.

In September 1940, I was again sent to Tideswell School. I arrived ready for trouble but nothing happened for several days. I was on the lookout for my assailant, then three of his cousins came at me, lead by the smallest of them. I could see they meant business; normally I would have ignored the smallest one, but he had something about him. He reminded me of a Jack Russell squaring up to a bigger dog. So as soon as he was in range, I hit him right on the bridge of his nose. He stopped and fell flat on his back. I hit the second one and the other ran away. Mr James, the PT teacher came running over; he knew trouble was brewing, but it was over before he could do anything. I went to help Alan get up, but he still wanted to fight till he could see I meant no harm, and we became good friends from then on.

Later in life, when I was first married, my new wife and I had taken the tenancy of a farm at Bredbury. We had had two wet years and been unable to get much fodder. Things were very tight, so when some gypsies wanted to camp and pay for doing so, it was a big help to us. And when I lost my wife after an accident they quietly got on with the farm work while I was in a daze of total shock.

One day some time later, a different type of traveller rolled into the farmyard asking for somewhere to park his caravan. He opened his window and said, 'Spraken zee Deutsch?' I answered, 'Nein.' He didn't speak much, saying his name was Hans Striger and he didn't have much English. He wanted a good clean place away from the other gypsies and was willing to pay. So we walked round the yard, at the bottom of which was an open cart shed with a concrete floor. His eyes opened with delight and more so when he looked round the other buildings and seeing inside were new loft floors; he wanted to rent one of them for a gym.

I asked him his name again; he looked blank, his face was like a tanned leather boot. I said, *'Now, while you're talking to me in my yard, what is your real name; from your dialect you belong somewhere not far away.'* So he replied, *'Clark Mellor, but keep it to yourself; the tax inspector is after Clark Mellor and can't find him.'*

He asked how much I would want for rent; I didn't know, so he offered £20 a week for his motors and caravan and a further £10 to rent a loft. A good worker on the railway or such was then earning about £10 a week so I was very pleased to accept.

He set himself up by cleaning the site up; he wasn't afraid of work and he started using the loft as a gym with a boxing ring, weights and such like. He invited me to join him and some mates for half an hour or so up there; he said it would do me good. The half hour soon grew into 2 or 3 hours. He disappeared towards the end of each week, paying me when he got back. I commented, *'You must have a good job somewhere.'* He replied that he had a sparring contract with Freddie Mills for so many hours a week. Freddie was one of our boxing champions then.

Clark taught me many things, to be faster, have better footwork and to ride punches. My father noticed a difference in me; he wanted to know what we were up to and have a look for himself. He was known to be handy with his fists when necessary, being very strong from working in the quarries and he would stand no nonsense in the Bagshawe Arms, or from anyone in fact.

Clark in later life.

After the second week of being with us Clark had to go to court over a driving offence and when he came back, someone else was driving; he'd lost his license. He asked me to drive for him, so I would be earning more money. But there could be trouble as well, his other job was wrestling. Some of his friends asked if I was part of the team; I found out they were a wrestling team called Joint Promotions who put bouts on nationally. As part of the setup, I carried a pair of saddlebags over my shoulder and wore a big hat as we showed ourselves off. I enjoyed being a part of this until he got his license back.

Some Staffordshire gypsy families stayed for the winter on a bit of rough but dry land and they came back each year. One day some other travellers came onto the site without asking and some of the genuine gypsies came to me asking if I knew about their new unwelcome neighbours. I said I'd seen them and was going to shift them off whereupon one of them said, *'Be very careful what you are doing and watch their women, they are more dangerous than the men.'* I thought about what he had said; I knew I would have to do it first time and fast.

First I got Maurice, who worked for me, to start the bulldozer and drive it onto some high ground about 100 yards from where the caravans were as a show of strength. I walked into the camp and a big rough man, obviously their leader, met me. *'Who has told you that you can camp on this land?'* *'The owner has given us permission.'* He replied. So I told him he was a liar, I owned the land and no-one else.

Things then happened fast and remembering the warning about the women being dangerous, I was keeping an eye on his woman standing in her caravan doorway a few feet away. Her right arm was sliding slowly up the doorpost and I spotted what she was reaching for - a knife which was stuck in the timber door frame above her head. I had to act quickly with her man and knowing she was going for the knife, I hit him much harder than I should have, right in the throat. As he went down, she'd got the knife and was coming; I grabbed her right wrist with the knife in the hand and swung her round at the same time squeezing until she dropped it, then pushed her down to join him on the floor.

Then I said to her, *'Look after him, he's a good man.'* The hate drained from her face - I had no worries about her from that moment. But two of his mates were coming, I thought they were going to help him up but they came straight at me. The first one caught me a blow on the chin, but I rode it and while he was looking to see what effect his punch had had I hit him twice, hard enough to start him reeling and another good one to the chin felled him. The second man stopped, held his hands up and said, *'No boss, you're too good for me, I'm off.'* In half an hour they'd packed up and gone.

Mrs Smith, one of the genuine gypsies called me to her, *'Let me look at your knuckles.'* After a good look, she rubbed some of their home-made healing cream on. *'There, your hands will be even harder now.'* She turned my hands over and said, *'I can see danger ahead - a giant of a man under a chestnut tree. When you meet him, treat him with great respect.'*

Next morning, old Bob Braddock came across to the farm and congratulated me on the performance, but he said, *'We have not seen the last of it, mark my words.'* Nothing happened for 3 or 4 days, then two gypsy boys came into the yard and said breathlessly that some men were in their camp looking for me. Edwin wouldn't tell them where to find me, so they beat him up. Edwin was the best man in the gypsy camp, so I knew the newcomers must be good.

After I had changed my boots, I went across to see what was going on. I could see a big stranger sitting on a 5 gallon oil drum by the camp fire. He got up from his seat and came at me with his head down to head butt me. This was like a dream come true because from being a boy and working with animals, we used to feed the sheep with bags of hay and with a bit of persuasion a tup lamb will attack the bag, but if at the last moment you move the bag, he'll go straight past. Of course as they get older and wiser they turn and come charging from the other side, so you have to remember you've been standing behind the bag now and move smartly or he'll butt the legs from under you.

As the man came charging at half the speed of a ram, it was easy at the last moment to side step and as he went by, with both hands together I hit him a rabbit punch behind the neck. He went down head first into the gravel without even putting his hands out to save himself. He got up after a moment or two with his arms flailing like a windmill, but I was too agile for him. I hit him hard in the face and he went down again. Then one of his mates came; he did manage to hit me on the chin but it was only a glancing blow and didn't do much harm. I kept him at arms length, then hit him twice with my right then in his throat with my left. He went down holding his throat and trying to breathe, but I was tiring; if there were any more of them, one would knock me down.

Two came out of the small crowd which had gathered. My heart sank but at that moment a voice behind me said, *'One of them is mine; this is my camp you've come onto causing havoc.'* It was Tom Lee. Quick as a flash Tom hit the one nearest to him, I can still hear his jaw break to this day. The two left standing collected their mates up, put them on the back of the wagon and carted off.

A year later Bill Braddock, a good travelling gypsy, came walking into the yard early one afternoon to ask would I take 3 or 4 of them out for the night; they would call for me about 5 o'clock and would fill my petrol tank. I thought they were being over generous, and that there was something in the wind.

We set off for Buxton, then took the A515 towards Ashbourne, turning off for Via Gellia and then at Pikehall, turned for Parwich, stopping in the centre of the village. Then I saw it; a big spreading tree with a man like a mountain stood near. Mrs Smith's warning came back to me, *'Treat this man with respect.'* So I walked over to him and introduced myself. *'Claude Fearns from Bredbury; these travelling lads stay on my land.'* He took me by the hand, saying he'd heard of me. His hands were like number 4 shovels. I held my own on the handshake. *'Don Lownds, my name, the Fighting Blacksmith.'* Then he took a hammer and struck the anvil ringing it like a bell.

A crowd was gathering and he shouted out, *'Ladies and Gentlemen, we have an interesting line up for you tonight. We have some new blood, so to speak, some professional, some amateur - you'll have to judge for yourselves.'* Now these so-called friends I'd brought down had said I was their top man but I took care not to put my name down on the blackboard which the competitors put theirs on. Don looked at the list, *'There are two names missing, maybe they are shy; so at the end of the evening they will fight me, either one at a time or both together!'* the crowd laughed at his remarks.

I don't remember a lot about the fights; it was bare-knuckle, stripped to the waist. I thought some of them were play-acting to the crowd. As the evening drew to a close, Don announced that the two newcomers would meet each other for the last bout of the night.

When our turn came, the anvil rang. Now I had never hit anyone without due cause and I felt like a fish out of water. We danced around play fighting for the crowds benefit, then in the second round, Don bellowed, *'Ten pounds for the winner.'* My opponent turned into a mad thing and came at me, meaning business. I warded him off twice but on his third attack, I turned sideways to him and hit him with my right, well it was more him running into my fist than a punch, but it stopped him in his tracks, then his knees buckled and the remainder of him curled into a heap on the floor.

Don bounded into the ring, held my right arm up and declared me the winner. He said *'I could see what was coming two minutes before. Come and meet some of my friends.'* One was a big raw-boned man over 6 feet tall with wide shoulders. He leaned over to shake my hand, I offered him my left, the right one was still hurting and I didn't want to risk getting it crushed in his shake. He looked me in the eye and said, *'I could see the outcome of your fight long before the end; I could not have done better myself.'* I asked him if he was a fighter. *'Only when I have to and that is how you should remain. You'll have to put one or two more appearances in, but as soon as you lose a fight, pack it in, that's my advice. Big H is my name; I know all the local travellers, some good, some bad, but the Evans, Braddocks, Lees, Togoods, Price and Smiths are a good lot.'*

That was the end of my first day; at later dates, I had three more bouts, coming out OK but the fifth one was different. Big H wandered amongst us before the fight began and as he passed by me he said, *'You're down for losing this one today; the man you have is a villain. Don't be tempted by easy targets or he'll make a mess of you-good luck.'*

There were several fights before ours and when we met I could see he was a veteran. He was good but not as agile on his feet as me; age was on my side. I managed to keep out of trouble then he started offering easy targets if I was foolish enough to take them, but I was watching his hands ready to counter attack. By now he was getting tired and offered a target with his hands down by his side, so then I hit him with a right and left, shaking him. He came back but I was too handy on my feet for him to do any damage. I hit him whenever he got close enough and by the seventh round he was done for; when I hit him again, he reeled, went down and stayed there.

Don bounded into the ring to declare me the winner. I saw a chance of some play acting and instead of giving him my right arm to hold in the air, I took up a defensive stance saying loudly, *'I do not have to fight you as well do I?'* He was taken completely by surprise. Before he had time to collect himself, I hit him twice. The crowd roared but it was the first and last time I had any chance of hitting the Master. I had not hit him as hard as I could have done and

Tideswell

he knew it. His response was too fast for me to do anything about it. It was a good job he knew I was play acting, he only hit me in the ribs but it took all the wind out of me and I finished up on the floor gasping for breath. He pulled me up and held my arm up as the winner of the last fight, but I was loser to him and that was the last fight I had.

Fifty years later, I was in the Bluebell at Tissington. At the other end of the room was a funeral party and standing at the bar were three men. I thought the big fellow looked familiar. Then it dawned on me - Don Lownds. I asked the barman to take him a drink from me. He looked across to see where it had come from, acknowledging with a nod and after a while he came across and greeted me with a gentle fist in the ribs. *'Does that ring a bell?" 'It does!' 'I've got the right man then.' 'You certainly have!'*

'Tidza' Band (Tideswell) at Wormhill. Blessing of the Well 1950s.

Pauline Jackson

Mum and dad had a rented farm at Marple-about 38 acres; then when my brother Phillip was about 15, they sat round the table and asked him, *'Do you want to farm or not?'* and he said, *'Yes, I do.'* So they put their shirt on a farm at the foot of Kinder Scout, near Hayfield-Ravens Leach Farm. They hadn't got a penny; it was a 42 acre farm and cost £6,200 then in 1963. It was that bad winter and we moved up there in the March. I was five and they moved on a cattle wagon and I went on the bus with my grandma and the dog.

Dad was working part-time for Bateson Trailors; he had started off with Ken Bateson. Mum was of Irish descent, she came from County Cork. I'm very proud of my Irish roots.

I was at Hayfield school when mum said to dad, *'I could do with a bit of pin money really, Donald.'* He said, *'Well, if you want to start bottling a bit of milk, you can deliver to these few houses down at the bottom of the lane.'* There were 6 little cottages, so she decided to put some milk up into bottles and see if she could sell it and she did; I think that's where I've got my milk round skills from, my mum.

Pauline with grandad & Phillip.

So then dad left Batesons and they bought some cows and my brother became the cowman; he got some very good quality stock over the years.

I had some happy days at Hayfield School and happy memories of the Hayfield May Queen. I used to dress up and be the Beefeater or the Crown Bearer for 5 or 6 years; I never wanted to be the Queen.

I started delivering milk from about 8 years old with me dad; I used to go every Saturday morning. In those days we used to milk the cows, we'd be finished by 8 o'clock then start and bottle the milk from the night before and that morning. It was only cooled, nothing else done to it. When we first went to the farm, there were shippons in a courtyard, 15 cows in one, 8 in another and we used to carry the milk over to the dairy in units. Then when bulk tanks came in, we built a new parlour in 1972, one of the first abreast parlours in the district then, because people were tending to go for the herringbone parlours. It was right at the side of the dairy, so the milk came out of the cows and only went 10 or 15 feet and then onto the cooler before the milk tank. So there was no mauling of the milk, no pasteurising or homogenising like they do now. I think the taste of milk has left it now to a certain extent. That's when milk was milk and of course if you left it, the cream rose to the top, which you don't see now.

We used to bottle it, cap it and put it on the truck, then go and have our breakfast, then off we'd go. We had an old J4 van with a side door; there were 2 seats and in the middle was the engine and on top of that was a place to sit for children; well, you weren't supposed to, but you did. Sometimes my brother came along and I always ended up sitting in the middle because I was the youngest. It was always warm and one day as we were going down the road with the milk, I said, *'It's getting a bit hot here dad.'* *'Are you alright?'* *'Yes, but it feels hot.'* The battery was underneath and it had shorted across and set on fire. It was on fire underneath my bum!

There was another occasion when dad pulled up outside the shop to go in with the milk and

Dad and Uncle Jim.

a little lad had pulled up behind him on his bike to go for the papers. Of course dad never saw this bike and backed straight over it. When he saw what he'd done he said, *'I'm sorry, here's half a crown for a new wheel.'* The lad took the money and bought some sweets and never told anyone what had happened to the bike, but it all came out in the end.

So we started off delivering around Birch Vale and then grew into New Mills. I helped until I left home to get married and then living at Wardlow, I decided to start a milk round off my own bat. I just went round with some cards one day; I was milk recording then, going round the farms, so it did start to clash a bit with the milk round. So when I saw a job advertised at Bagshaws for a Monday morning at Bakewell market and I didn't have to start till 9.30, I thought I could get the milk round done before that, which I still do and I've been there about 15 years now. I work on the calf section now and the stores when there's a Thursday sale. I started in the old market when we had about 400 calves, selling the continental calves separately from the English calves. In that building then it could be freezing cold, not nice in winter. We only get about 100 calves now.

I buy my milk in bottles from Cox's at Great Longstone and from Peak District Dairy at Tideswell, which is Walkers. All produced and bottled on the farms. Cox's used to do Green Top (unpasteurised) until a few years ago, that's why I went there, because people wanted it. I was always a big believer in it and I think things may come full circle and it will be allowed to come back into fashion.

Thomas William Brocklehurst

I was born in November 1924 at Cow Close Farm, between Birchover and Stanton in the Peak. Father was born at Sheldon and took the tenancy of Cow Close Farm in 1922. One of the first things I remember is of going with an uncle to Rowsley Station with a horse and cart to cart brewers' grains back; it took half a day to fetch 15 hundredweight of grains.

Another time, we went with the pony and trap, the de-luxe version of the milk float with seats at each side, wooden wheels with solid rubber tyres and lamps on. You paid 5 shillings a year license for it. We went to grandfathers at Woodbine Farm, Sheldon. This would be 1926 or 7. All the village was rented from Chatsworth then and they were nearly all relations of ours. We went to church at 2pm, then visited up each side of the street, having a drop to drink at each place. They were supposed to be teetotal, but home-made wine didn't count! A drop here and a drop there, we'd get back about midnight in all sorts of weather. That night it was snowing and they put me in a clothes basket under the seat, fast asleep.

Sometimes I stayed with granddad; they were a bit short of room so I had to sleep with him. I was only small and he started snoring. I said, *'Grandad, granddad, you're snoring.'* He says, *'What! Snowing.' 'No, snoring'*.

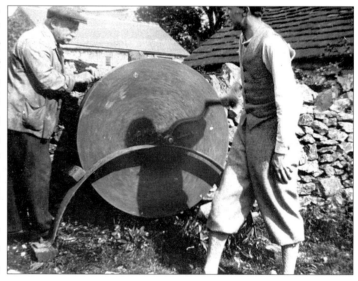

Between having the pony and trap and getting a car of our own, we used a taxi. The Silver Service Garage at Darley Dale had an Austin, a beautiful one and this smart young man came from there to Cow Close, took us to Sheldon, went back to Darley Dale, then came back at night to pick us up and take us home. All for 15 shillings.

It was mixed farming at Cow Close; there were Shorthorn dairy cows which father graded up to pedigree Friesians, sheep, pigs and poultry. We grew oats, kale

Edwin Brocklehurst, Sheldon carpenter, is on the left.

and cabbage, turnips and mangolds which had to be hoed first by hand - singling. We'd buy up to 10,000 cabbage plants out of the market; all had to be dibbed in by hand and each one had to have a handful of fertilizer put near it and in a very dry time we had to take churns of water and go and give each one a drop of water round the roots. The corn was cut with a binder; a nice job on a nice day. Neighbouring farmers came to give a hand at thrashing time and we went back in return; there was always a houseful of people for meals.

There were lots of callers or reps; Flewitts of Ashford, Cauldwells of Rowsley, Johnsons of Darley Dale and national firms. Grocers came; Burgens came every week and Ormes fortnightly for their orders and delivered a few days after. The reps probably came for 20 or 30 years and became family friends. Also Broughtons, drapers came round; Mr Curtis with hardware, Alexanders from Buxton Road, Bakewell came round with cakes, sweets and biscuits. All the butchers from round about used to deliver; there were up to 10 butchers in Bakewell at that time.

Above:
Stacks on
Sheldon Moor.
The round ones
are corn stacks.

Left and below:
Old Sheldon.

Uncle George
thatching.

Right:
Thomas William
Brocklehurst Snr
broadcasting oats.

Below:
The Brocklehurst
family.
Lunch on Sheldon
Moor.

A lot of stock was driven to market but calves, sheep and pigs were taken in the float, the working equivalent of the pony and trap with a net over the top. The horses put up at one of the pubs; we used to put up at the King's Arms on Buxton Road; a lot of the pubs had stabling facilities then. There was a good vet in Bakewell, Mr Marrison; he charged a guinea a visit and the doctor charged 10 shillings.

Before the war, there was father, one man and a youth on 200 acres; a lot of the land was rabbit infested, there was no money or inclination to do anything with it in the depression, then war started and it altered altogether. We got another man, then in 1941 the first land girls came - they were thrown in the deep end, the first two we had were from a dress shop in Sheffield without any training whatsoever, but with patience they turned out very well. One, she hand-milked 18 cows on her own sometimes. Also gangs of land girls came; they were bought on a lorry, 30 or 40 at once to do the weeding; we had extra arable then, 10 acres of potatoes and more corn. Lady Manners School let the scholars off for potato picking. We also had our own soldiers when they'd got a bit of spare time, then later in the war, loads of German and Italian prisoners.

We first had a tractor in February 1941, a David Brown VAK1. I'd spend all day on it, ploughing, discing, all the jobs on 200 acres. You could sit in the rain all day with it running down your neck inside your coat. I've been so cold sometimes that I got off and walked up the side with one hand on the steering wheel and jumped on at the end, turn it round and then jump off again to try and warm up.

Jean joined the Land Army in 1943. Arriving in Bakewell, she went to the War Ag - the wartime Ministry of Agriculture offices - for instructions as to accommodation and where to go the next day. I was going in and passed them on the stairs going up to the office, I was asking for some help on the farm, so next day they arrived at Cow Close Farm. That's how we met. When she joined the Land Army, she was thinking she might go to Devon or Cornwall, but landed up just down the road at Bakewell. They were with us a week or so, setting potatoes etc. After that she did all sorts, mole-catching around Sheldon, ending up with the Beeby family at Over Haddon. They had a milk round around Bakewell and Ashford. In the '47 snow they had to strap the milk churns onto a five bar gate and drag it down to Bakewell with a horse where someone met them and took the milk round for them. Then they had to do their jobs and the milking when they got back; it was after midnight when they finished. You couldn't see any walls, you just ran over the top of them.

We decided to get married later that year and lived in a cottage next to the farm until in 1955, when we got the tenancy of High Field Farm at Ashford where we moved to with our son, Neil. We had the tractor which dad had purchased in 1941 and which we kept until 1990. Implements were mainly converted horse implements and as time went by we were able to upgrade and expand and we did some contracting for farmers and the County Council.

When we first came to Ashford, sheep washing was done on a regular basis, paying the Parish Council 6d a score for sheep washed to pay for the upkeep of the pen. We were paid more per pound for washed wool compared to unwashed but as time went by the price gap narrowed and the extra weight of unwashed wool made up for the extra money for washed wool, so we gave it up. We gave a demonstration in 1974 in well dressing week using six sheep and crowds of people came to watch.

In granddad's day they divided the sheep from the lambs and took them down to Ashford, amidst a lot of bleating. They put them in the pen, then after they'd been in the river they ran up onto a grassy piece to dry off. The flocks of sheep were queued up down the road. They got

mixed up going back up to Sheldon but would peel off at their own farm to get back to their own lambs. They kept Lincoln Longwools at that time and father relates cutting 27lbs of wool from a tup, the ewes averaging 14lbs a fleece.

Milking at Sheldon in summer was done in the fields by hand and father said the worst time was when it was wet and windy, when the three-legged stool sank into the ground, and the rain running off the cow and down your arms and legs.

Milk fever was often fatal then; grandfather once sat up with a cow all night which the vet may have given up on. They gave it half a bottle of whisky and piled hay and rugs on her to get her to sweat and she recovered. It was his habit to give a newly calved cow some scalded maize or oatmeal and half a pound of black treacle made up into 2 or 3 gallons of warm water.

The milk was taken to Longstone station by horse and float to go on the train to Manchester. There were

some bad journeys in winter when two horses had to go to pull the float through the snow drifts and back up the dale, which is very steep in places and as it is north facing, ice stayed on it. Going downhill, Grandfather sometimes had a struggle, no matter how he tried, to keep things straight, the float slipped sideways until the horse was facing uphill and it was difficult to get right again. Studs were put in the horseshoes so that at least the horse could stay on its feet.

They once had a young horse, a three year old and when he got used to going downhill, he would go flat out. It was all they could do to keep the churns on the back of the float and stand on the back to keep the shafts high, put the brake on and let him go. One time the roadman left off work and stood aside when he saw them coming, watching in amazement as they went flying by as most horses held back in the britchband and went down the hill steadily.

On the way to the station, they went on Longstone Lane, in those days called Shady Lane. At the side of Picacrow buildings there was a swampy piece of land where bog gas lay. One night as they passed the buildings, the horse caused a spark on the limestone road which ignited the gas and lit all the bog up - it is known as 'will-o-the-wisp'.

The farmer provided the churns, his name was stamped on the metal of the 17 gallon churns. Some of the dairies, when overdone with milk, would return no churns for several days.

Oats were sown broadcast, 18 stones to the acre, though some farmers sowed 24. Father could sow an acre in $^3/_4$ of an hour. The hay and corn stacks had to be well thatched on Sheldon Moor or they would have been blown all over the fields.

Grandfather liked trees and on some of the land he farmed planted sycamore trees in the

AT COW CLOSE FARM, BIRCHOVER.

Sid Bird, Rose Brocklehurst, Ivy Beardsall (land girl). FW Brocklehurst below.

Jean Brocklehurst in 1944.

Bob Wright and Tom Brocklehurst.

At Cow Close.

Tom and Jean Brocklehurst at High Fields Farm during the foot and mouth epidemic of 1967.

Arthur (far left) and Tom Brocklehurst (2nd from right) with friends at Cow Close.

Sheep washing at Ashford c.1920.

Tom and Neil, with dad on the binder behind.

corners of the fields for shade and shelter which are still there. A lot of the fields had old lead rakes through them; old workings and filled in mine shafts, in one place 10 mines in half an acre. There were the remains of an old cock-fighting ring by one mine. Some of the old pits held water and they once lost a lot of cattle. The water was analysed and found to contain a lot of lead, so the pits had to be fenced off.

Grandfather said that the long 'Once-a-Week' plantation was so called because when the mines were busy, a fair with stalls of meat and clothes was held there once a week. Also a blacksmith's shop where the miners had their tools sharpened. Cornish miners were among the men coming to work in the area and it was said that beds were never cold in Sheldon as the men worked in shifts and occupied the beds in turn.

On bonfire night, along with the fires, gunpowder could be obtained from the miners and long trails laid and lit at one end and the flames went running along. Some older boys had a 'cannon' about 9 inches long with a half inch bore fastened to a block of wood. Powder was put in, then wads of paper, then stones; all rammed in just like the real thing. A bit of paper in the priming hole was lit and they quickly retired round the corner. Surprisingly, father didn't remember any accidents!

When the first war broke out, horses were commandeered. Many farmers going to Bakewell show a few days after war was declared had to sell their horses, whether they wanted to or not. Luckily grandfather had left his at home, getting a lift with a neighbour and so he managed to keep his trotting horse.

Cheese press and bake stone in the Devonshire Arms, Sheldon.

Ian Cox

My grandfather, Harry Cox came up from Somerset to work on the railway in the early 1900s; I think he was a signalman. He also had an interest in farming, so as well as working on the railway, he rented a bit of land at Little Longstone and kept a few cattle. After a year or two, he'd got a bit more land and the railway found out about it and gave him an ultimatum; that he must either give up the farming and work on the railway or give over. Well, that was what we were told, which seems unusual.

At that time, Church Lane Farm at Great Longstone came up for rent; it was owned by the Wright family of Longstone Hall. So he put in a tender for it and got the tenancy. After a year or two, he married a girl from Little Longstone called Rose Taylor and they had two sons, Bert and Bill. Bert was oldest by three years and when Bill was born, Rose contracted pneumonia and died a week later. This left grandfather to bring up my father, Bert, and Bill was brought up by a lady in the next village.

Later on, Harry got married again to Annie Clay from Youlgrave and they had a daughter, Edith who later married Arthur Barratt, a renowned cattle-dealer from Chapel-en-le-Frith. At the time, he would be one of the biggest dealers in the country.

During the 1918 flu epidemic, Harry contracted the flu and died which left Annie with Bert aged 16 and Bill 13. They didn't think that they could manage to carry on the farm, but an elderly retired farmer in the village called Oliver Johnson took them under his wing and said that he'd help them as much as he could. They managed to make a go of it, buying the farm in 1928.

In the 1920s they started a milk round, going round the village with horse and cart with churns in the back and measuring out what people wanted. They had a quart measure, a pint measure and a half pint measure. One of the other farmers in the village used to go round before them under-cutting by a ha'penny a pint to try and get the sales.

During the 1940s, they started putting the milk into bottles. This was straight from the cow; just cooled. In winter the churns were stood in troughs of running water outside the house here; but in summer it had to be tipped into a pan and run over a surface cooler in the dairy.

Uncle Bill suffered with ill health; asthma and other breathing problems, so although they were in partnership, he couldn't do much heavy work. So generally he did the milk round and father did the farming which worked quite well until winter when in the bad weather Bill would be poorly and father had everything to do - milk the cows, bottle the milk, deliver the milk, wash the bottles, feed and clean out and milk again.

So in 1950 Uncle Bill retired and I wasn't just old enough to help so they decided to give up the milk round and sold it to Mr Middleton at Monsal Head which went under Middleton's Dairies. He only delivered pasteurised milk and people who were used to untreated milk decided they still wanted that and asked if they could fetch it from the farm; so they started coming with jugs, cans and bottles and we sold it from the door for a number of years until the Public Health decided that that wasn't hygienic and it would have to be sold in sealed and measured bottles.

That has carried on until today except in 1984 more regulations came in saying untreated milk couldn't be sold to canteens, offices and the like where people might not know they were drinking it. So we bought a small pasteuriser because we supplied the canteen at Thornhill's Poultry Packing Station further up the village with 80-100 pints of milk a day; which would have had to have stopped. So we sold both pasteurised and Green Top milk.

Eventually in 1999 the cost of testing the Green Top milk became too high for it to be

The Threshing Team about 1955.
George Redfern, Bill Cox, Bert Cox, Graham Wild, Frank Garrett, Stan Birds.
Front: Terry and Roger Cox

Cox family Great Longstone in the 1930s.

Harry Cox, Billy Cox and Bert Cox 1914/15..

viable; I think the cost and regulation was a back door way of stopping it. It cost us £65 a time to have it tested, so we gave up the Green Top.

We have customers who come from Sheffield, Chesterfield, Stockport and all around. One customer has been coming from Bakewell for 45 years; he comes on a Friday morning for 12 pints which last him for a week and he's never had a pint go sour yet. People come and help themselves from the fridge and leave the money on the slab; it might sound a bit casual but it works very well, 99% of people are very honest.

We used to wash all the milk bottles by hand, a time consuming job. Then we saw an in-crate bottle washer advertised at a farm sale near Chesterfield, so we went to have a look at it. It looked a decent machine, but we saw one or two other dairymen there and thought we hadn't much chance of buying it; it would make more than we'd

Ian

want to pay. When the auctioneer got round to selling it, he stood there and couldn't get a bid for it. My brother bid £10, the auctioneer took another bid for £15 then knocked it down to us for £20 which we thought was a right old bargain. We've had it for about 35 years and it must have washed hundreds of thousands of bottles.

The farm is opposite to the church and sometimes we get problems with traffic when weddings and funerals are taking place. Some years ago, one Saturday morning in wintertime my brother went up the road with the tractor and rota-spreader loaded with muck for the fields. There was a wedding and a white Rolls Royce was delivering guests.

Eventually it came with the bride and her father. As they got out and walked up to the church I could hear a rattling noise up the road. It took me a minute to realise that it was my brother coming back and with it being winter, he'd got the radio on and the heaters blowing and obviously couldn't hear that he hadn't switched the spreader off. I couldn't get out quick enough and as he came past the Rolls Royce, he covered it in a fine mist of cow muck. He pulled up quickly, jumped off and had a word with the driver, then came panicking into the dairy saying, *'Do you know what I've done?' 'Yes, I do. Tell him to back in and we'll wash it off.'* Luckily there was time to spare, the driver backed to the dairy and sat in the car reading the newspaper while we frantically cleaned it up. After a few minutes it was done except for some stains on the white ribbons. The driver said, *'That'll be alright - they won't notice that!'*

Robert Pheasey

My father started the haulage business, H. Pheasey in 1934 at Ashford. He was an engineer and used to work at McEwan's Garage in Bakewell and at Taylor's Garage. He started by cutting the back off his car to find a job for his brother who'd been laid off at the chert mine in Bakewell.

When I was born, we'd got 8 milk lorries, then he accumulated 3 more rounds from the Milk Board. It was all milk lorries until 1954 when there was de-nationalisation and he bought haulage vehicles from British Road Services at Darley Dale, eventually having 19 vehicles.

In wartime, dad and uncle went to Bakewell to sign on at the recruiting office but when they found out that they drove milk lorries they told them to go home and they'd send for them if they needed them, which they never did because milk was a priority then.

We ran milk from all round here to Sheffield, Mansfield, Chesterfield, Manchester and sometimes to Tarporley in Cheshire, all contracted to the MMB. We were paid so much a month based on gallons of milk transported and mileage and then at the end of the year they'd ride round with you and do a survey and assess your accounts and if you'd lost money, they made it up. So it wasn't a great job but you never lost.

There were good points and bad points with the Milk Board but they were the ruling body, whatever they said, that was it, you couldn't reason with them. They could look at a map and say what was to be picked up on what, yet there could be lorries crossing. At one point at Monyash, there were 4 milk lorries crossing.

We did a lot of corn as well from Manchester down to the local feed mills, John Flewitts at Ashford Mill, Cauldwells at Rowsley, Baileys at Matlock and Bakewell. Two lorries went to Manchester and left the churns at the dairy, then went to the mills at Trafford Park. Then we'd send a Chesterfield lorry that was back early down to Manchester to fetch empty churns back. In winter the corn job was five days a week. It was long hours and hard work but even so it was enjoyable, there wasn't the pressure and rush of nowadays, the money and paperwork.

Uncle Les Rowland was a cabinet maker, so he was the joiner of the business and we used to build the milk lorry bodies for Mycocks at Buxton, Adam Morton at Buxton, Shimwells at Youlgrave, Lincoln Gee at Reapsmoor, George Bull of Tideswell and of course ourselves.

I started going on the lorries in the early sixties though I liked being in the garage on repairs the best. Most of the farmers were great and very friendly, if they could help you they would, in the snow and bad weather they were very good, they'd bring the milk for miles to meet you. I remember going into Peak Forest one day; we managed to get three lorries in - we hadn't been for about 4 days because of snow - and the dairy at Wythenshawe stayed open for us because they needed the milk, there'd been none through from around Buxton.

Dad started with the big 17 gallon churns, but when I was on they were mostly 10 gallon steel churns. They were near enough 10 stone when full and some you had to lift on yourself from the floor and then double-deck them especially round Wormhill and Weston where it was winter milk; you could nearly double your load, in fact we had to put an extra lorry on. There was one farm had Channel Islands at Great Longstone and they had 12 gallon churns which went to a separate dairy at Wythenshawe. At the dairy you unloaded the churns onto a conveyor belt, then they were tipped. In later days they were tipped into a tank with a weigher on, so you tried to keep each farmer's churns in order.

Around Edale was a nightmare, 52 collections on that round. They were mainly at the side of the road but odd ones you had to go up to the farms on the hillside and right up to Barber Booth as far as the road went and on the same round up the Snake Pass - up to the Snake, turn round and pick up on the way back; down to Ashopton and all round there. They were mostly hill farms, probably sending two churns; the big farms were round Parwich, there were only 9 collections on that round, it was the biggest load we had, the main farmers being the Bunting family. One of the Buntings at Low Moor farm used to have their own milk lorry and take it to Mansfield Co-op. Dad bought the round off them but you had to have sanction from the Milk Board. When we finished churns in '73, we were down to about 4 vehicles then from 11 but they wouldn't let us have tankers. We arranged for Mycocks to have what we'd got left but at the last moment the Milk Board stepped in and said, *'You can sell them the lorries, but we're having the milk round.'* And they ran their own tankers from a depot near Chesterfield. They did the same with Shimwells.

It was the Express Dairy at Sheffield that first started with a tanker in 1964 in this area with a little old Commer truck with a tank on it, with a pull-start engine for pumping the milk on. They had a lot of trouble with it, but took 5 of the collections on our Parwich run on the first day, so we were left with half a load. I heard of a couple of accidents collecting the milk from stands on the roadside; one near to Longstone picking up and a lorry smashed into them; there was milk everywhere.

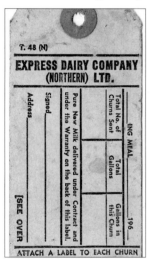

Another was one of George Bulls on Tideswell Moor in the fog, roadside collecting. The driver heard the lorry coming and jumped off over the wall - a good job because it smashed the lorry to bits; we helped them out for a while until they got fixed up with another truck. You wouldn't want to be doing it nowadays.

The core of drivers were very reliable, but you'd get odd ones let you down especially with it being 7 days a week; there was never a day off. I used to get fed up sometimes; it was always on a Sunday morning, a driver would ring in sick, but they'd leave it till 9 o'clock and it was always me who had to go and you were an hour and a half behind to start with. Some of the dairies liked to be done for noon and on the Monyash run you had to go down to One Ash Grange and Cales Farm; you could be an hour on the pick-up and gates to open in places too.

In the end me and my brother said to dad, *'We're not doing it any more.'* We were running miles for the remnants left from the tankers. We ran haulage after that, a lot of work into Kent and paper from a mill there back to Manchester to Deansgate - all the newsprint for the Daily Express, People and Daily Mail. But then for the main job going south, we were undercut so dad said, *'Enoughs enough, we need an increase not a cut.'* So we finished as a family business in 1982. The company which undercut us went bankrupt 2 months later!

Bert Cox at Great
Longstone.

BELOW: Oddfellows at Taddington.

BAKEWELL RURAL DISTRICT FOOD CONTROL COMMITTEE.

THE BUTTER (MAXIMUM PRICES) ORDER, 1917.

NOTICE IS HEREBY GIVEN that the Local Food Control Committee have fixed the MAXIMUM PRICE applicable to the sale by retail in the area of the Bakewell Rural District, of BRITISH-MADE BUTTER from Creamery, Factory, or Farm, in Rolls, Bricks, or Prints (½lb.), at:—

2s. 4d. per lb., including all charges for credit on delivery.

such prices to remain in force from the 15th day of NOVEMBER, 1917, until otherwise determined by the Committee.

NOTE.—No retailer shall sell any Butter at a rate exceeding by more than 2½d. per lb. the actual cost to him of the Butter sold.

Infringements are summary offences against the Defence of the Realm Regulations.

By Order.

GEO. ALLSOP,
Executive Officer.

Local Food Office.

Dick Dale

I worked at Dowlow Quarry after the war; I went well-boring with a machine with a mast on driven by compressed air. It used 9 foot stems threaded at each end; the first stem had a drill bit on the end which you bore down with first. Then you reversed the motor, uncoupled it and sent it up 9 foot and hold it up while you put a fresh stem on to the drive, then bring it down to the one already bored, screw it in and set off again for another 9 foot. Then keep going till you've done 96 foot right to the bottom of the quarry bed. Drill these holes 12 to 16 foot apart, a dozen in a row. Then the explosives were put in the bottom, coupled up with cabling to a battery and the holes filled up with dust. When it was set off, it lifted the quarry face out.

On a foggy day, you never saw anybody but jackdaws; you couldn't even see the edge of the quarry. While I was there, someone was doing the same job and putting a stem on. It had been raining and he'd got a bag round his shoulders. The motor at the top is rotating onto the thread - what happened? - it got fast with the bag and throttled him.

Before the war, I'd been working with a bloke, Jack Yates, a fitter. They were putting a dry house up to tip stone in to dry overnight, to dry the muck off it. I had to climb these girders to fasten the girderwork. He says to me, *'Yer want see t' boss, climbin' up theer - ex 'im fer more money.'* I did do. Packet come Friday night, penny an hour extra. Job came to a close and the buggers cut the penny off again!

When I was well-boring, I had a caravan with a fire to do a bit of cooking. The boss came one day and said, *'We'll have this caravan decorated up - I'll send a dumper up for it tonight.'* They fetched it to the fitting shop and it was done lovely, black on the outside, cream on the inside. Saturday dinnertime, I knocked off at noon. I next came to work as daylight was breaking; I thought, *'That caravan looks different.'* It had been painted over. DICK DALE'S DINER - HOT DOGS - MUGS OF TEA - CAKES. The boss, Mr Jackson always had a walk round. He got to the top and stopped dead, he was flabbergasted. Monday morning, the dumper came again, up with the caravan, down to the fitting shop to be painted up again.

Rotary well-drilling rigs.

Dangers of Quarrying - Claude

I left school during the early part of the war and started to work on the farm with father. Doing it part time while at school is one thing but full time is another and we weren't working on any projects; I wanted to build an old car into a tractor by using two gear boxes in line to give extra towing power giving a choice of 18 speeds. But we did build a four-wheeled harvest trailer which we entered into Bakewell show when it started up again, in a competition for something manufactured locally. We came 2nd behind Binghams of Smalldale with Joe C Bamford of JCB fame coming third with a hand-powered tipping trailor.

So, as I wasn't happy working at home, dad got me an engineering apprenticeship at ICI quarries. On the first morning I walked down to the post office to meet the bus which came every day to take the quarry men, only this morning it didn't come because it was snowing. So the little group of us walked up Wormhill, round by Hargate and down the fields towards the kilns through the snowdrifts in the dawn half-light to Tunstead Quarry.

One of the first jobs was to join the men out of the workshops, get some besoms and shovels and sweep the snow off the points on the lines because the kilns had to be kept fed or they could take a fortnight to get back into production. They have to be charged night and day every day of the year, even Christmas. If heavy snow occurred enough to stop staff travelling to work, those already manning the kilns stayed on until they were relieved. In 1947 at Blackwell Mill, staff didn't get relief for 72 hours. Food was a problem but after 36 hours the Manchester Central-London St Pancras Express managed to get through, dropping food parcels off as it slowed down going past the kilns and the Buxton junction.

Enough stone was the next problem, the narrow gauge wagons loaded with stone would run out after 40 hours or so, so in a lull in the weather every man except the burner turned out to load stone from the stock pile. After 2-3 hours all available empties would be filled and run down to be used as needed. Stock stone was for any emergency when sufficient stone could not be got from the quarry face and there could be 6 months worth stockpiled.

I remember as we left work at lunchtime on Saturday during the war, a bus load of white-collar workers of various professions had come to load stone from stock onto the wagons and put them back in line. They managed this job alright with not having to break any of the stone, just load it. At Tunstead, the coal wasn't a problem, it was stored in bunkers and two loaded railway wagons stood in the unloading shed.

I worked from South shops, Tunstead; I had to carry stuff about quickly to and from workshops. I was quickly learning about good

A diesel Simplex loco.

Clearing the snow.

jobs and bad jobs; most were dangerous, some more than others. One of the jobs was to pick up stones which had fallen off the trucks, creating danger zones. We put one of the filler's numbers on the truck and then filled it - he would pay us 1s 3d which was half the price he would have been paid for filling a truck with stone.

I learned about safety using explosives and went to night school at Buxton where I really struggled, not being able to write. I started working on the locos, helping to strip heads off and de-coking - the drivers didn't stop them at lunchtime because they had to be started by hand. I worked five and a half days a week earning 3d an hour, 11s for the week. Gunpowder came in hundredweight sacks and when they were empty we took them home and boiled them at the end of the wash to boil the tallow out of them. You boiled them off a time or too till they were like linen; they made beautiful pillow cases.

We ate and sheltered in a cabin when heavy rain made it dangerous at the quarry face. The cabins were built of railway sleepers and had an egg-shaped stove with a ring round the top where you could put your brew can and make toast round it.

As often happens, there was a bully who ruled the roost tormenting first one and then another. I had been left alone, probably being the youngest but then my turn came to receive his attention. I can see him now; he always wore his hard safety hat. I took no notice

Hand-picking 1950s

of him and he got abusive then threw a piece of hard toast at my face. Surprisingly it drew blood. That did it! Springing from my seat, I grabbed my tea can with a pint of tea in it - it all happened so fast; I swung the can over my head and brought it down hard onto his helmet - it felt as though I was lifted off the ground. He fell backwards; his reign of terror was over, but the story of his downfall was not.

The first accident that I was involved in was when a man called Harold Pheasey was filling stone and instead of clearing the clay and waste into another truck, he was putting it in a heap behind him. There had been blasting this day and some stones fell off the top and one particular one landed on its end and then fell over trapping Harold on his clay pile. There was a big loco jack which I made a dash for; normally two men carried it with a bar through it. Speed was of the essence, we were frightened of more stone falling. I managed to pick it up and run with it. As I got near two men took it off me. I'd have collapsed with it if they hadn't. Luckily, we got him out.

In wartime some girls were brought in to work in the quarries. Joan Malthouse, from Millers Dale was one and she was set to work driving a dumper to take clay to tip it down the waste tip. It may have taken a day or two to load it perhaps with two tons. She drove up to the edge, set the tipper up, put the brakes on for it to empty but the clay was stuck in it, it held and pulled her over the edge and she was killed. She hadn't been taught to read the tip face when it was dangerous. Within a month the same thing happened with another woman so they took women off anything mechanical - a bit heavy-handed as some of them were quite competent.

On another occasion a man was popping, that is drilling big lumps of fallen rock and putting explosives in to break them down. On this occasion the getter had blown some rock down from higher up the face and there was a heap of rock. This particular rock had been drilled, charged and fused, then blasting time had come and everyone had run for the shelters. The holes should have been counted and you should listen for the charges to go off. This time he'd miscounted, the stone had slid down and probably dragged the fuse out. It was laid on the quarry floor for a day or two with the drilled hole face down then one morning the first thing he did was go and drill it but it had already got a charge in the middle and so when he started, the explosives were triggered and he was killed.

Popping.

Opening No 2 cutting at Tunstead, May 1934.

Brian Oven

My father, Jack went to Rock Lodge, Priestcliffe in 1931, as a tenant; it was owned by grandfather, Isaac Lomas, who had bought it off Mellors. It was just under 40 acres, then we put another 90 acre to it in early wartime. The rent was £27 10s.

Father had started work at 13 at Tideswell, at Brook Bottom Weaving Mill. He must have had something to do with weaving because he showed Margaret how to do the joining knots, that is splicing the wool. From there, he went to the quarry at East Buxton, working in the kilns. That would be in the late 1920s. He was on the staff grade of pay, so he was guaranteed a wage and they always found them something to do. When they were slack at one time, he was sent up to what is now Tunstead, with a pick, shovel and wheelbarrow, baring, which is taking the topsoil off. He often said to the children, *'How would you do at Tunstead today with a pick, shovel and wheelbarrow?'*

Mr Gould at High Cliffe, Priestcliffe Ditch.

Grandfather Lomas originated from Reapsmoor and he farmed at Crossroads Farm, Blackwell until 1937; he died in 1939. When he retired, Uncle Bob, Robert Lomas took over Rose Farm at Priestcliffe and Uncle Percy Longden took over Crossroads Farm. They were half brothers; Percy was born before gran was married.

Grandfather used to go back to Reapsmoor, visiting and call at the cheese factory there for some cheese and he wouldn't have it unless the mice had been at it. Whether it was because that was a good cheese or whether it was cheaper, I don't know. But they always used to say mice took to the best cheese.

Gould family.

I was born at Priestcliffe and went to Priestcliffe C of E school. Originally, the school was at Priestcliffe. There is a Schoolhouse

VALUATION of Tenant-right for which
Mr. Leonard Smedley is entitled to be paid on quitting
the Priestcliffe Ditch Farm, Taddington, in the County
of Derby, by his Landlord J. Gyte Esq., or his ingoing
tenant Mr. T. S. Gould.

Lady-day, 1920.

————————————

In Yard,
        Harness pegs in stable,
        14 Neck chains in cowhouse,
        Gate and timber forming door to
            cart house,

An Allowance for labour on the carting and
    spreading of manure in meadows Housefield,
    Pretty Close, and Low End.

An Allowance for ploughing in Long Lane field.

The unexhausted value of purchased feeding
    stuffs consumed on the Holding during the
    last two years of the tenancy.

————————————

SALE
at
HIGH CLIFFE FARM, Nr TADDINGTON.
for
MR. T. S. GOULD.
Sale,   17th, March,   1930.

W. S. BAGSHAW & SONS,
AUCTIONEERS, LAND AGENTS,
SURVEYORS AND VALUERS,
UTTOXETER.

Sale at High Cliffe Farm.

49	Chain harrow	2	2	6	65	Milk scyes		4	6
50	Manure tank	1	1		66	Milk churn)			
51	Plough	1	3		67	2 ")	2	5	
52	Horse hoe		3		68	Egg box		6	6
53	Tined harrows	2	15		69	Medicines	1	1	
54	Swingletrees		3		70	Cow truss		6	6
55	Wood harrows		18		71	Pt cask treacle		9	
56	Cart	20			72	Ropes			3
57	Butter churn		5		73	"		4	
58	Press)				74	Cart ropes		5	
59	Yokes)		1		75	Hd stall etc		2	
60	Cheese vats		3		76	Plough pads & lines		18	
61	Milk bucket		7	6	77	Bridle		16	
62	"		7	6	78	Set harness	2	7	6
63	Measure can		15		79	Back band & chains		5	
64	Milk bucket		5		80	" "		3	
		30	9	6			9	13	3

Mr Gould.
Priestcliffe Ditch.

The snow in 1947 around the council houses at Priestcliffe.

Priestcliffe in the snow.

Nellie Gould at Priestcliffe.

Farm in Priestcliffe, but that's nothing to do with it; that belonged to Pursglove School in Tideswell. The school was in a field at the side of Rock Lodge Farm. That field is always known as Schoolers Yard or Scholars Yard. You can still see the wall and where there's been a gate. It was closed in 1847

and moved to the top of Taddington, where it stayed as Priestcliffe School until 1950, when it became Taddington-Priestcliffe C of E. School.

I went there until I was 11; it was in wartime. I remember there were two landmines dropped at Priestcliffe in the early 1940s. It was night-time, but I never woke, I slept through it. They went off, not quite on our land, leaving craters; we still have pieces of shrapnel. Although I never woke, it made me stutter - that's what they put it down to, the shock of the explosion.

At Priestcliffe.

The building roof had to be re-slated, it was shattered. Several properties had to be done; the house was alright though. Sellars from Bakewell did the re-slating and they gave me some nails and laths, and I mustn't let postman see them, so I went round back of the house with them.

Grandfather Oven lived in Tideswell; he was a quarry worker, but he did a bit of farming as well. He once went to Wales, buying store cattle in the spring of the year. He went in a collar and tie. He was stopping overnight and he couldn't get the collar and tie off, he slept in it; his wife had fastened it up. Several of them went from Tideswell in the spring for store cattle and they would be railed to Miller's Dale.

Wilde family at Taddington View, Priestcliffe.

Mr and Mrs Oven 1929, at Crossroads Farm.

We milked until the 1970s; our milk never went on the train, it was always picked up by road. George Bull, from Tideswell picked it up.

There was mains water in Priestcliffe from the late 1800s; it would have been by public subscription. It came from the back of the Waterloo and was a poor supply. Priestcliffe, being lower, was turned off every day so that pressure would build to feed Taddington village. We had a long stretch of pipe, so ours never really went off; we never went short in the house, but we had to be very careful with water. In a dry time, we had to go down to the river in Miller's Dale and fetch it in a tank, a hogshead, which we filled with buckets.

Out in the grounds we had a barn. I used to go and fodder the cattle there before going to school. I'd be about 10; it was before I went to Buxton school. I goes up these steps, opens door and there's a tramp asleep. I don't know what I did then, if I fed the cattle or not but ever after I'd take the dog. At the bottom of steps, get hold of dog and drag it up steps, open the door a little bit and push dog in first.

Margaret Oven

My dad, John Fearns, was always known as Jack. He was born at Cowdale and went to school at King Sterndale. When he left school, he went working as a farm labourer for Bart Bagshaw, near Crowdicote and various others. Granddad had a farm at Shireoaks near Chapel-en-le Frith, so then dad went working for him. He was courting mother and wanting to save up and get married, but granddad wouldn't give him any wages, so he used to catch rabbits and my mother would sell them in Buxton for him. She was Winifred Shelley and worked as a cook at Boden Hall for the Lauder family - they were related to Harry Lauder.

Shireoaks wasn't far, so they could meet up, but then when mother left and went into Buxton, dad was flying about on a bicycle at all hours to see her. He'd had enough, so as he had a brother, Uncle Jim, working on a farm near Burton on Trent, he went with Uncle Charlie on the motorbike to see if Uncle Jim would go back and work for granddad. In the end, he got fed up and just left and went down to Burton, got a labouring job and some digs and married mother. Uncle Jim went back working for granddad for a while, till he got fed up and eventually dad went back because granddad was desperate.

As a family, we'd moved about in the Burton area to various farms and were very settled on a farm near Repton. They didn't want dad to leave; he was waggoner as well as doing all sorts of other jobs. So we came to Shireoaks and I started school from there. We had to walk down the fields to where the railway ran across to the Cowburn tunnel, where we crossed over a bridge and went up to Malcoff, where we caught a taxi into Chapel. Going over the bridge, if a train came, all the steam and smoke came up and the engine drivers and the guard always waved at us, they got to know us; it was like *The Railway Children*.

In 1947 mother was taken ill and had to go into hospital, but they couldn't get the ambulance to her, they had to carry her on a stretcher down the fields. Up the drive were 13 gates, they couldn't go that way, it was full of snow. They got an army truck to take her so far.

I was left as a 5 year old, father had got the farm to look after, he was out looking for sheep. He'd got Uncle Herbert there and my brother who is 5 years older than me and the bad weather. I can see mother on the settee now; it was appendicitis, which perforated. She was lucky to survive and was in the Royal Infirmary at Stockport, closed now, for several weeks.

Margaret and John at Shire Oaks 1947.
Left: Mum, Carol Salt and Margaret, 1951.

I was taken to Edale, to my Uncle Norman's and Aunt Doris looked after me. One thing that sticks in my mind is that I'd got chilblains bad and couldn't go outside, so I used to sit in the window; they had lovely window seats

Carnival party in 1952, in Peak Dale band room.

Shireoaks from Malcoff.

Carol, mum and Margaret.

and I used to play with the cats; I've always been a cat person. Uncle Norman had a 'tash and I'd seen him trimming it, so this cat had its whiskers trimmed. I don't live it down to this day.

I also remember going for potatoes to the barn and the cockerel attacking me. I hate cockerels. It didn't work out with granddad and so we moved. Dad took the tenancy of Heath Farm at Smalldale; it was the Duke of Devonshire's farm. When they moved, I was sent to Uncle Charlie's, the Bagshawe Arms at Wormhill and I went to school there for a month. Then when all was settled, back to Smalldale. Why I was always the one sent off, I don't know.

Granddad also had a farm, The Burrs at Chelmorton and in earlier times, he worked in the quarry, stone filling. Either Ashwood Dale or Cowdale quarry. He was a big union man, so he had to work to keep everybody satisfied. He would tell the foreman there to leave his trucks ready and he would see that they were filled before morning. So after they had finished hay-making or whatever, the family went back with him to see that the trucks were filled.

Choosing the Queen 1951, Peak Dale.

Choir Festival time at Peak Dale School.

Angela Taylor WORMHILL & DISTRICT YOUNG FARMERS CLUB

During the winter of 1951 the club was set up and met weekly at Wormhill Village Hall. Claude and Muriel Fearns were the main instigators from being in Chapel YFC, with Bernard Mycock, local farmer and father of four daughters, and Cliff Hancock, who worked for Staffordshire Farmers at Millers Dale Mill, helping to get it up and running.

At Wormhill Well Dressing 1951. Young Farmers Michael Ryder, Bill Gregory, John Mycock, Geoff Gregory.

My father, Geoffrey Pickford who worked on a farm in Wormhill was also one of the founder members of the club. He always told me that there were a lot of good-looking girls at Wormhill, and where the girls are the young lads will soon follow. At its height the club boasted 41 members who attended regularly and they were regular winners at county events. They won the county shield four times and the

Ted Mosely, Brian Oven, Geoff Pickford, Geoff Gregory, Neville Longden,
John Mycock, John Howe, Bill Gregory.

ABOVE:
Wormhill YFC club prize
giving in 1952.
Mr GH Drewry, agent to the
Duke of Devonshire,
presenting.

RIGHT:
Buxton YFC Rogation Sunday
at Wormhill 2002.
Louisa Fotherby, Jenny Taylor,
Louise Taylor, Stephen Mycock,
Anna Taylor, Alison Taylor,
Glyn Colley.

Stone-walling competition at Hargate
Hall late 1950s.

junior shield seven times.

The youngsters who attended became proficient in many tasks as varied as ploughing, stone-walling, root-singling and poultry trussing. Some of the members were particularly good at public speaking. My own daughter won the Derbyshire Advertiser Cup the same trophy as her grandfather won in the 1950s. Many of the members went on to be successful farmers all around the district.

Poultry trussing competition at County Rally in 1953, Wormhill YFC. Jean Mycock on right.

Annie Taylor

I can remember walking to a dance at Taddington institute with my younger sister Mary during the war. We were living at Monksdale Farm at Millers Dale then. I was 16 and Mary two years younger. We walked up long lane to the top of Priestcliffe Ditch and then on to Taddington.

The search lights were eerily lighting up the sky and the noise of aeroplanes going over was constant it was quite scary for two teenagers. My father Ben Gregory, insisted that he met us at the institute and walked us back home safely.

The Taylor family at Old Hall Farm, Wormhill.

Bibby's trip to Port Sunlight in the 1950s.

A good old-fashioned party. Thought to be Christmas at Taddington.

A little parachuting - Claude

In the late 1940s I went abroad on several missions as an engineering specialist. The need to train REME specialists to jump was to get them to anywhere in the world fast. We were put through intensive physical training and learning how to fall; then after several weeks we went to Woodford to jump from a 100 foot tower, dropped on a cable controlled by air-brakes. It was very scary being dropped on such a thin cable. We then moved to a platform beneath a barrage balloon, first from 100 feet, then 200, then 300; getting ready to jump from an aircraft. But out of 30, there were only 12 of us left; the others couldn't meet the standard.

The order came in the post to report to Failsworth. After being welcomed by the CO we were fed and given a packed lunch. We collected our gear, fell in and were given a pep talk before being marched out to an RAF coach. We headed north past Lancaster up Shap, which was then a notorious road. When we reached the summit, we started the steady downhill to Carlisle and onto Gretna, Dumfries, Castle Douglas and onto Stranraer, down to the docks.

The bay was full of all kinds of craft including flying boats - Catalinas and Sunderlands. We were taken into a lecture room for a final briefing and then with our stomachs in our mouths, marched out to the landing pier to where a huge aircraft was waiting. It was on the edge of dark, the moon was getting up, we moved on board, the doors closed and the four giant Rolls Royce engines roared into life. We moved slowly at first, then it got bumpy until I thought we would be shaken to pieces, then suddenly the shaking stopped - we were airborne.

Nobody said much, we were all thinking about what was ahead. We had always known where we were going to land off towers and balloons; this was different-not knowing where or into what we were going to land or how fast.

After what seemed like hours, a voice came over the speaker *'Ten minutes to drop.'* Then *'Five minutes.'* Then *'Two minutes - get ready. One minute - Zero.'* And in turn out we went, all of us terrified. As I went through the doorway the cold hit me more than anything. It was free-fall for five seconds, then as the chute opened, you got the sensation of being dragged up in the air again. That didn't last long, it was quiet and peaceful; I looked down to see where I was going to land-then I saw it, it looked like a ten acre reservoir. I'd always been frightened of water since living at Shireoaks. There was a reservoir with concrete sides and iron railings, on the way down to the Breck and my parents drilled it into us to keep away from it. And here I was heading for the middle of one.

It was a moonlit night and I could see the waves. We were trained and equipped for landing in all kinds of terrain; I had flares and was wearing a 'Mae West' inflatable jacket. As I got lower, I could see small waves going before the wind. When I was only ten feet from the surface, I realised it was not water but a field of green oats about 3 feet tall. I was ready to land in water as we had been trained to and it was too late to

change my stance to prepare for a hard landing. I hit terra firma hard, damaging my right knee badly. When rescuers came to me, I was laughing; they thought I was in shock. I told them I was a farmer and mistook green oats for water. That knee troubled me for over 50 years until the leg was amputated above it; now there is only the memory.

John Claude Fearns 1927-2008

Sadly Claude passed away before this book was published, so I would like to pay tribute to a great friend who I have learned so much from these last few years. It was working with him to get his book *Claude: White Peak Memories* published that started it off and the series of 'Around' books have all sprung from that. We have met so many wonderful people as we have gathered our material.

Claude was unique, a larger than life character; a gifted storyteller and a fount of knowledge and commonsense wisdom about country life, and many other things that he had learned in the diverse fields in which he had been involved.

He gave over 65 years of public service in many ways in many communities, culminating with 12 years as a member of the Peak District National Park Authority, representing the 26 parishes of Staffordshire and Cheshire. He was always willing to help people out; he was passionate about the people and countryside of the Peak District. He has left a wonderful legacy of memories and will not be forgotten.

SH